Karen.Kevin.Joshua Sutton
30 Waine Close
Mount Pleasant Heights
Buckingham MK18 1FG

CIM Companion:
marketing fundamentals

CIM Publishing

CIM Publishing

The Chartered Institute of Marketing
Moor Hall
Cookham
Berkshire
SL6 9QH

www.cim.co.uk

First published 2002
© CIM Publishing 2002

All rights reserved. No part of this publication may be reproduced in any material form (including photocopying or storing in any medium by electronic means and whether or not transiently or inadvertently to some other use of this publication) without the prior written permission of the copyright holder, except in provisions of the Copyright, Designs and Patents Act 1988 or under the terms of a licence issued by the Copyright Licensing Agency Ltd., 90 Tottenham Court Road, London, England, W1P 9HE.

This book may not be lent, resold, hired out or otherwise disposed of in any form of binding or cover other than that in which it is published.

Series Editors: John Ling and Mark Stuart.

Applications for the copyright holder's written permission to reproduce any part of this publication should be addressed to the Editors at the publisher's address.

It is the publisher's policy to use paper manufactured from sustainable forests.

British Library Cataloguing in Publication Data
A CIP catalogue record for this book can be obtained from the British Library.

ISBN 0 902130 98 6

Printed and bound by The Cromwell Press, Trowbridge, Wiltshire.
Cover design by Marie-Claire Bonhommet.

contents

	page
Study guide	1
Session 1 Marketing – an introduction	10
Session 2 First stages in marketing planning	28
Session 3 The marketing plan	42
Session 4 The marketing mix	63
Session 5 Product	76
Session 6 Price	96
Session 7 Place	108
Session 8 Promotion	122
Session 9 Service marketing	138
Session 10 ICT and monitoring marketing effectiveness	151
Session 11 Marketing in differing contexts	162
Session 12 Marketing in international and virtual contexts	175
Glossary	186
Appendix 1 Feedback to Case Studies	194
Appendix 2 Syllabus	202
Appendix 3 Specimen examination paper	208
Appendix 4 Feedback to the specimen examination paper	215
Appendix 5 Assessment guidance	225
Index	231

Study guide

This Companion is written to complement the recommended core text by Dibb, Simkin, Pride and Ferrell, *Marketing concepts and strategies* (4th European Edition), published by Houghton Mifflin. It aims to offer you support as either an individual or group learner as you move along the road to becoming a competent and proficient marketer. This is a process of learning that has two important elements:

Understanding marketing concepts and their application

The following Sessions have been written to highlight the concepts you will need as you start to understand marketing fundamentals, what marketing can achieve, and how it is implemented. The concepts are described briefly and concisely to enable you to cover a range of key material at first stage level. It does not attempt to be fully comprehensive, so to further develop your understanding of the concepts introduced here you should read widely from:

- The recommended course text (readings are specified for each of the Sessions in this book and shown in Table 3.).
- Other texts and workbooks listed in the syllabus reading list.
- The marketing press and national newspapers.

Other comprehensive marketing textbooks are detailed on the reading list for the syllabus, and provide a wider context for the concepts explained in this Companion, and provide more Case Studies and examples to illustrate marketing in practice. The syllabus can be found in Appendix 2 of this Companion.

Developing the skills to implement marketing activity

Equally important in the journey towards marketing excellence is the acquisition, development and refining of a range of skills that are required on a daily basis by marketers across all industries and sectors. These transferable skills hold the key to the effective implementation of the marketing techniques explored in this Companion. The focus of the practical activities contained in this book is on seven key business skills for marketers:

- Using ICT and the Internet.
- Using financial information and metrics.
- Presenting information.

Marketing Fundamentals

- Working with others.
- Improving and developing own learning.
- Problem solving.
- Applying business law.

The first four of these key skills are linked to the activities shown in Table 1.

Improving and developing own learning is achieved by undertaking the projects at the end of each Session.

Problem solving is achieved through the Case Study and questions at the end of each Session.

Applying business law is achieved by a special project linked to Session 12.

Using this Companion

The syllabus for Marketing Fundamentals has been broken down into twelve Sessions, each of which cover approximately the same proportion of the syllabus content. Every student brings with them to their studies different levels of experience; as a customer, from previous studies, or possibly from working in marketing or sales. You should therefore be aware that although you may need to spend considerable time on unfamiliar areas of the syllabus, you are likely to make up this time when studying other more familiar areas.

Each Session has a series of short activities, which you should try to complete as you work your way through the text. These will help you check your understanding of the material. Brief feedback is provided at the end of each Session so that you can compare your answers.

At the end of each Session there is also a Case Study and a series of related questions. Some of these have been taken from past examination papers, so you can use them to help you prepare for this type of activity in your exam. Try to complete these without reference to your notes, or the Session text, and then compare your answers to some of the key points given at the end of the Companion (Appendix 1).

Finally, you will see that there is a Specimen examination paper (Appendix 3). This can help you with your revision, exam technique and preparation. Allow time nearer your actual exam to complete the paper under exam conditions. Give yourself three hours of uninterrupted time, and complete the paper without reference to your notes or the study material. When you have completed the exercise, you can compare your answers to the notes in Appendix 4. If either your approach to the exercise, or the comparison of your answers highlight any areas of particular weakness, you should refer back to the text and re-read the relevant Session, together with the chapters of the supporting textbook.

This Companion's structure and content follows the syllabus order, as the Marketing Fundamentals module follows a standard "process" which is in itself logical in its "flow".

Marketing Fundamentals

Table 1 – Key skills

	Using ICT and Internet	Using financial information and metrics	Presenting information	Working with others	Applying business law	Improving and developing own learning	Problem solving
Session 1	Case Study 1.4, 1.5		1.4	1.3	1.5	Project activities	Case Study
Session 2	2.1		2.1	2.2	–	Project activities	Case Study
Session 3		3.1, 3.4		3.3	–	Project activities	Case Study
Session 4	4.2		4.1, 4.3		–	Project activities	Case Study
Session 5		5.4	5.2		–	Project activities	Case Study
Session 6	6.3	Case Study 6.1	Project B	Project A	–	Project activities	Case Study
Session 7	7.3		Project A 7.1	Project C	–	Project activities	Case Study
Session 8	Project B 8.3	8.4	8.2		–	Project activities	Case Study
Session 9	9.2		9.3	9.1	9.2	Project activities	Case Study
Session 10	10.1	Case Study			–	Project activities	Case Study
Session 11	Project B		11.1		–	Project activities	Case Study
Session 12	Project C 12.3			Project B	Special project	Project activities	Case Study

Table 2 – Web sites

Please note – these web addresses were active at the time of going to print. The owners of the web sites may move specific pages, so you may need to visit the home page of the site, and search for specific information via an alternative route.

CIM	
www.cim.co.uk	The Chartered Institute of Marketing.
www.connectedinmarketing.com	Everything you need to know about e-marketing.
www.cimvirtualinstitute.com	Key learning tool for CIM students.
General Marketing	
www.new-marketing.org	Research updates into new marketing issues, customer segmentation and repercussions for marketing practitioners.
www.wnim.com	What's new in marketing.
Advertising	
www.adslogans.co.uk	Online database of advertising slogans enabling marketers to check whether a slogan is already in use.
www.nielson-netratings.com	Details on current banner advertising.
www.ipa.co.uk	Institute of Practitioners in Advertising.
www.asa.org.uk	Advertising Standards Agency.
www.warc.com	Advertising and marketing related data, trends, etc.
Direct Marketing	
www.dma.org.uk	Direct Marketing Association.
www.theidm.co.uk	Institute of Direct Marketing.
E-marketing	
www.connectedinmarketing.com	Everything you need to know about e-marketing.
www.shopping.yahoo.com	Browse retail sites.
www.ecommercetimes.com	Daily e-news.
www.amazon.com	Customer-focused operation.
Events	
www.e-bulletin.com	Guide to exhibitions, events and resources.
www.venuefinder.com	International venue and event suppliers directory.
Sales Promotion	
www.isp.org.uk	Institute of Sales Promotion.

Marketing Fundamentals

Public Relations	
www.prnewswire.co.uk	UK media monitoring service – reviews mentions in all media types (print, online publications and broadcast).
www.prsource.co.uk	PR and marketing information sources.
www.ipr.org.uk	Institute of Public Relations.
Personal Selling	
www.iops.co.uk	Institute of Professional Sales.
http://mkt.cba.cmich.edu/jpssm/	Journal of Personal Selling & Sales Management (American).
Marketing Research & Intelligence	
www.mrs.org.uk	The Market Research Society.
www.keynote.co.uk	Market research reports.
www.verdict.co.uk	Retail research reports.
www.datamonitor.com	Market analysis providing global data collection and in-depth analysis across any industry.
www.store.eiu.com	Economist Intelligence Unit providing country-specific global business analysis.
www.mintel.com	Consumer market research.
www.royalmail.co.uk	General marketing advice and information.
www.ft.com	Financial Times online newspaper and archives.
www.afxpress.com	Business news plus industry trends.
www.caci.co.uk	ACORN classification of residential neighbourhoods.
www.isi.gov.uk	Information society site with details of government projects, pending legislation etc.
www.worldmarketing.org	World Marketing Association.
www.statistics.gov.uk	Office for national statistics (UK).
www.homeoffice.gov.uk	Research development statistics.
www.business.com	Business search engine.
Legislation/Codes of Conduct	
www.wapforum.org	Industry association responsible for creating the standards for Wireless Application Protocol (WAP).

Table 3 – Background reading

The following references are suggested background readings for each Session. It is suggested that you undertake this reading before studying the relevant Companion Session.

Session	Reading from core text: Dibb, Simkin, Pride & Ferrell, *Marketing concepts and strategies* (4th European Edition), Houghton Mifflin.
Session 1	Chapter 1 – An overview of the marketing concept. Chapter 23 – Implementing strategies, internal marketing relationships and measuring performance. Chapter 24 – Managing ethics and social responsibility.
Session 2	Chapter 2 – The marketing environment. Chapter 6 – Marketing research and information systems. Chapter 21 – Marketing strategy.
Session 3	Chapter 7 – Segmenting markets, targeting and positioning. Chapter 22 – Marketing planning and forecasting sales potential. Chapter 23 – Implementing strategies, internal marketing relationships and measuring performance.
Session 4	Chapter 7 – Segmenting markets, targeting and positioning.
Session 5	Chapter 8 – Product decisions. Chapter 9 – Branding and packaging. Chapter 10 – Developing and managing products.
Session 6	Chapter 18 – Pricing concepts. Chapter 19 – Setting prices.
Session 7	Chapter 12 – Marketing channels. Chapter 13 – Wholesalers, distributors and physical distribution. Chapter 14 – Retailing.
Session 8	Chapter 4 – Consumer buying behaviour. Chapter 5 – Organisational markets and business-to-business buying behaviour. Chapter 15 – Promotion: an overview. Chapter 16 – Advertising, public relations and sponsorship. Chapter 17 – Personal selling, sales promotion, the Internet and direct marketing.
Session 9	Chapter 11 – The marketing of services.
Session 10	Chapter 23 – Implementing strategies, internal marketing relationships and measuring performance.
Session 11	Chapter 20 – Modifying the marketing mix for various markets.
Session 12	Chapter 3 – Marketing in international markets. Chapter 20 – Modifying the marketing mix for various markets.

Table 4 – Marketing models

Models are used to simplify various complex situations or processes. The text in the Companion Sessions refers to a range of appropriate marketing models, but does not reproduce these as they can be found in the core textbooks. The references for these are supplied in the following table.

Session	Marketing Model	Reference: Dibb, Simkin, Pride & Ferrell, *Marketing concepts and strategies* (4th European Edition), Houghton Mifflin.
Session 1	■ Marketing concept.	■ Page 9.
Session 2	■ Macro/micro-environment. ■ Marketing audit.	■ Page 60. ■ Page 710.
Session 3	■ Marketing planning cycle. ■ Organising the marketing unit.	■ Page 691. ■ Page 721.
Session 4	■ Socio-economic classification. ■ Market segmentation approach. ■ Basic elements of segmentation. ■ Segmenting consumer markets. ■ Example of life cycle stages. ■ ACORN. ■ Segmenting b2b markets. ■ Target market strategy.	■ Page 130/131. ■ Page 206. ■ Page 209. ■ Page 211. ■ Page 215. ■ Page 217. ■ Page 224. ■ Page 231.
Session 5	■ Levels of product. ■ Product mix and depth. ■ PLC. ■ Brand equity. ■ NPD. ■ Product deletion. ■ Product adoption.	■ Page 254. ■ Page 256. ■ Page 258. ■ Page 273. ■ Page 299. ■ Page 312. ■ Page 462.

Session	Marketing Model	Reference: Dibb, Simkin, Pride & Ferrell, *Marketing concepts and strategies* (4th European Edition), Houghton Mifflin
Session 6	<ul><li>Channel intermediaries.</li><li>Types of channel.</li></ul>	<ul><li>Page 353/354.</li><li>Page 357/359/622.</li></ul>
Session 7	<ul><li>Pricing decisions.</li><li>Establishing prices.</li><li>Promotional pricing.</li></ul>	<ul><li>Page 573/575.</li><li>Page 589.</li><li>Page 603.</li></ul>
Session 8	<ul><li>Push/Pull strategies.</li><li>Channel sales promotion.</li><li>Uses of advertising.</li><li>Criteria for advertising.</li><li>AIDA.</li><li>Topics for press releases.</li><li>Elements of personal selling.</li></ul>	<ul><li>Page 472.</li><li>Page 538.</li><li>Page 483.</li><li>Page 488.</li><li>Page 499.</li><li>Page 509.</li><li>Page 524.</li></ul>
Session 9	<ul><li>Classification of services.</li><li>Dimensions of service quality.</li></ul>	<ul><li>Page 326.</li><li>Page 331/332.</li></ul>
Session 10	No specific models.	
Session 11	<ul><li>B2b channels.</li><li>Extended marketing mix.</li></ul>	<ul><li>Page 622.</li><li>Page 631.</li></ul>
Session 12	<ul><li>Levels of involvement in international marketing.</li></ul>	<ul><li>Page 74.</li></ul>

Session 1

Marketing – an introduction

Introduction

This Session introduces the concept of marketing, and starts to explore its role in creating customer value. It also looks at how marketing has evolved over the years. Achieving a marketing orientation is a long-term process and needs a lot of hard work and commitment – we look at how it can be achieved, and at the barriers that can get in the way.

> **LEARNING OUTCOMES**
>
> At the end of this Session you will be able to:
>
> - Explain the development of marketing as an exchange process, a philosophy of business, and a managerial function.
> - Recognise the contribution of marketing as a means of creating customer value and as a form of competition.
> - Appreciate the importance of a market orientation to organisational performance and identify the factors that promote and impede the adoption of a marketing orientation.
> - Explain the role of marketing in co-ordinating organisational resources both within and outside the marketing function.
> - Describe the impact of marketing actions on society and the need for marketers to act in an ethical and socially responsible manner.
> - Examine the significance of buyer-seller relationships in marketing and comprehend the role of relationship marketing in facilitating the retention of customers.

What is marketing?

The term "marketing" means many things to many different people. It has existed as a concept for as long as people have traded goods with one another, and so has a very long history. In this section we look at the three main ways it is viewed – as an exchange process, as a business philosophy, and as a managerial function.

Marketing as an exchange process

Marketing is concerned with trade. One person has something that is wanted or needed by someone else. Before money was invented, farmers were often those producing a surplus, and their goods were taken to market and bartered or exchanged for cloth to turn into clothes, or pots and utensils to use in cooking.

The farmer with more than enough for his family had a surplus that had a higher value to someone else. However, he gained something of value for himself in return through this mutually useful exchange process. Now, of course, it is money that is exchanged for goods, and the value that companies gain is measured in terms of profit – the surplus funds they have after covering the costs of production and running the business. Before the industrial revolution this exchange process was usually on only a small scale.

Marketing as a business philosophy

Not every organisation is marketing oriented – putting the customer and their needs at the centre of everything they do. In the past many more organisations have concentrated on the technology of the product, on sales, or on the production process.

Henry Ford famously said about the cars his company manufactured, 'Customers can have any colour as long as it is black'. Ford concentrated on production. The company was production oriented, in fact they were one of the very first to use production lines, favouring efficiency and productivity over gaining greater understanding of their customers.

A product-oriented company concentrates on developing their product, believing that a good, high-quality product will sell itself. However, even the highest quality, lowest priced, most innovative product, will struggle to gain market share if consumers do not know about it, do not need it or even want it!

An organisation that is sales oriented will rely on its salespeople to sell its products. Sales targets for the week, month or year are the main focus for the organisation. This can work well with very basic products, so long as salespeople are well trained, and make every effort to identify ways in which their product can meet the customer's needs. However, if you have ever been persuaded to buy something you didn't really want or need, you will appreciate that a company that relies on this technique will find it difficult to build customer loyalty. You will be very reluctant to return having been the victim of an aggressive sales technique! In addition, once customers are dissatisfied with a product because it doesn't meet their needs they might not refer others to you, and what's more, they might actually recommend their friends and colleagues not to purchase from you! This is applicable to both services and products.

Sales orientation should not be confused with a marketing-oriented company using personal selling as part of its promotional activity.

Marketing-oriented organisations recognise that customers are important. They concentrate on identifying customer needs and finding ways to satisfy and delight customers. Customer loyalty is important because research shows that the longer a customer remains with you, the more money they will spend with you. In addition, over time they may become ambassadors for your products and services, referring other people to you. Developing this kind of culture is not easy and requires constant reinforcing throughout the organisation. Everyone in the organisation must put the customer and their needs first – they need to "think customer" at all times.

Marketing as a managerial function

Communicating with customers is an important aspect of marketing, but marketing is about more than just brochures, web sites and customer databases. It starts with knowing who the customer is and what he or she is looking for. It involves research, planning, and pulling together all marketing activities, not just communications, to ensure that they are focused on this task. In a business with a strong marketing orientation, the customer is simply the focal point for everything.

There is also a difference between sales and marketing. In sales you are usually selling what you've got, your existing products and services (although a professional salesperson will try to match their products to a customer's needs). In marketing the emphasis is on understanding what benefits customers want, and may want in the future, then providing appropriate products and services for the salesperson to sell.

Marketing Fundamentals

Activity 1.1

1. Which of the following statements indicates that an organisation is marketing oriented?

    a. The organisation has a marketing department.

    b. The organisation has a marketing plan.

    c. The organisation has a marketing budget.

    d. The organisation is customer focused. ✓

2. The act of obtaining something of value from another party, and offering something of value to them in return is referred to as…

    a. Selling.

    b. Production.

    c. Exchange. ✓

    d. Manufacturing.

3. Which of the following shows that a company is adopting the marketing concept?

    a. The sales force meet their targets.

    b. The HR Department makes sure that all staff receive fair pay.

    c. The Managing Director makes a statement to the press about the success of the company.

    d. Senior management organises the whole business to ensure customer needs are met. ✓

Customer value and achieving a competitive advantage

The Chartered Institute of Marketing defines marketing as: 'the management process responsible for identifying, anticipating and satisfying customer requirements profitably.'

With the customer at the centre of all activity within the company, this process should achieve its goal. However, to develop long-term relationships with customers, companies need to deliver consistent customer satisfaction and create real value for them. The customer's perception of value is linked closely to the process of exchange. What will they get? How much will it cost them to get it – in terms of money, time spent searching, how their friends will view their purchase, and how it will make them feel about themselves.

Value for money has always been a factor in making choices between the products of one company, or that of competitors. Value for money is not just about cheaper prices – research has shown that individuals are often prepared to pay a little more for a better service. Companies that are seriously considering customer needs will think about the following issues as well as price.

Information – what information might prospective purchasers need when comparing them with competitors? How can they make this information freely accessible? Have they considered the features of their products and services and all the benefits that might be offered through them? For example, supermarkets often offer recipes, displayed against all the ingredients wherever they are on the shelves, not only giving the working customer ideas as to what to have as an evening meal, but also encouraging people to purchase more goods to make that meal!

Convenience – how can we save our prospective customers time in accessing our products? Can we use technology to help them access our products more easily? Can we give them a choice of how we contact them throughout our relationship with them? Sainsbury's have recently asked for volunteers to receive SMS text messages on their mobile phones – the important word here is "volunteer". They are using permission marketing to give their customers a choice of communication methods.

Association – what value might the customer gain from being "associated" with our brand? For example, teenagers are heavily influenced by peer pressure. Big name brands are popular, as teenagers feel they "fit in" when using them.

Added value – to make products easier to use, companies offer "technical support" through their web sites, or "care lines" to obtain information. Companies that are proactive in offering customers improved services for the same price, add value to their offering by showing a genuine interest in the customer.

In today's very competitive marketplace, where technology enables companies to produce very similar products, the "value" that a customer sees in your package of benefits can make the difference between the customer choosing you or your competitor. Careful research into what customers really want or need helps you to put the right package together and gain a competitive edge.

> **Activity 1.2**
>
> Imagine that you are marketing books from a shop in the High Street. What "value" can you offer to customers?

Marketing orientation

Actions involved in refocusing an organisation towards the customer include:

- Strong leadership from the top, with high-level executives building a customer philosophy into their business plans.
- Ensuring that all staff understand that the customer is at the centre of all business objectives.
- Persuading staff that changes in policies and processes are essential, and ensuring that they are implemented.
- Introducing an effective information system that will establish and track customer needs and wants.
- The organisation may need to be restructured to achieve co-ordination of all efforts towards customer satisfaction. Strong leadership and effective communication internally will help drive this change.

These actions are not easy to achieve, and may take considerable time. One of the biggest problems is persuading staff in departments outside of marketing of the need to change some of their overall policies and procedures.

Let's look at some examples.

Production department

Marketing, as we have already seen, is all about providing what the customer wants. Production staff may have been used to being able to manufacture large quantities of standard products. However, different customers may want small adjustments to the standard product, so processes may need to be changed to enable smaller quantities of customised products to be made.

Finance department

The finance departments' main focus in setting prices will probably be to meet all the costs and then add a margin for profit. Marketing is about looking at a wider number of factors in the marketplace, and then arriving at a price. Marketers may want to spread the costs of producing a number of products across the whole range, with some contributing more to profit than others. Don't forget many finance departments see marketing as a cost, not a source of income!

Sales department

Salespeople often work to short-term goals, aiming to achieve sales targets that are usually based on volume or value of sales made. They may be remunerated by a combination of salary and commission to encourage more sales to be made. Marketing emphasises the importance of customer satisfaction, and only selling products and services that are matched to customers' needs.

The commitment of all staff to a customer focus is important – the success of the whole business relies on its people. Yet most people like to work in a way with which they are comfortable. They need to be convinced that by changing they will see some definite benefit. Internal marketing is essential. This covers the activities and communication that the organisation carries out to create the environment that encourages people to "put the customer first".

Think about your own organisation and others that you know quite well. Consider:

- The extent to which market and customer research is carried out and how that information is used to improve the way the organisation meets customer requirements. For example, how have products and services been developed over the past five years? What improvements have been made that were in response to changing customer needs or identified customer dissatisfaction?
- How effectively customer requirements are communicated across the organisation and understood by people at every level.
- The management of quality and the understanding of the need to satisfy the internal and external customer. Are suppliers included in the "quality chain"?

- The importance put on customer care. Are all staff trained effectively, or is it deemed to be the responsibility of front-line staff only?
- The willingness of people in the organisation to make changes for the customer or meet specific requirements that may not be routine.

All of these factors contribute to the level of marketing orientation an organisation has achieved.

Activity 1.3

Talk to colleagues and your Manager about your own organisation, or one that you know well, and explore what they do to encourage and sustain a customer-focused environment.

Find out:

1. How much marketing research is done each year? Is there a department or an individual in a marketing research role?

2. Do they have a system to record and analyse customer complaints? What action is taken to make changes as a result of complaints received?

3. How do they communicate the importance of customer care to all their staff?

The role of marketing

In the last section we looked at the problems organisations face when trying to achieve a marketing orientation. Once adjustments have been made to the organisation's structure, and all staff work to move the organisation's focus towards the customer, marketing then takes on a number of key roles.

Customer "champion"

The person or people who really understand the customer group that the organisation is targeting. This understanding is then translated into action by representing the customer to all other departments and leading change within the organisation.

Researcher

A key role of marketers is research. Organisations need to be aware of what is going on in their environment, and take this into account when planning marketing activities. They also need to keep in touch with customers and their changing needs. Remember that marketers need to anticipate customers' future needs in order to keep ahead of the competition.

Planner

A marketing plan needs to be developed to show what part marketing will play in helping the organisation meet the objectives of its business plan. It will have its own clear objectives, and lays down the strategy it will take, with details of all the marketing activities that need to be undertaken.

Co-ordinator

Plans need to be implemented. Although marketers will not necessarily carry out all the activities themselves, they will take an active part in co-ordinating the activities that constitute the marketing mix (or 7 Ps).

Product – which products will we withdraw? Which products will we continue to offer? What new products do we need to develop to meet customers' needs?

Price – what pricing policy should we adopt? What factors impact on the way we price our products?

Promotion – which customers are we targeting? What message do we need to communicate to them? Which promotional tools are best for this purpose and this audience? When shall we use them, how many times, and over what period? Will the result justify the amount we have to spend?

Place – which channels will we use to get our products or services to the customer? Will we just use one, or do we need to use a combination? Which will be the most cost effective, and which will be most convenient for the customer?

People – who will be the best customer-facing staff for us to employ? What training do they need? How can we ensure they are professional in their attitude and appearance?

Process – what processes and systems do we need to put in place to make sure that customer satisfaction levels are met?

Physical evidence – how can we make sure that the company's image is appropriate for what we are trying to achieve? What are the premises like? Do we need staff uniforms?

Manager

Someone needs to take responsibility for monitoring progress on the plan. It needs to be reviewed regularly against the objectives set, and the budget allocated needs to be carefully managed. There is also a need to ensure that marketing activity stays within legal restrictions. For example, the Data Protection Act dictates the way in which organisation's can store, retrieve and use the customer data in their databases.

Ethics and social responsibility

If marketing is all about satisfying customer needs, then it seems common sense that the question of ethics and social responsibility should be seen as an essential part of marketing. Ethics are moral philosophies that define right and wrong behaviour in marketing. Social responsibility is an organisation's responsibility to minimise its negative impact on society as a whole, and maximise its positive impact.

With the intense competition that exists in most markets today, companies need to find ways of differentiating what they offer from their competitors. One way of doing this is by "putting something back" into society, and then communicating this to improve the company's image with the public.

To see examples of this in practice look at www.sainsburys.co.uk/social/ and www.heinekencorp.com and follow the link marked 'Responsibility'.

Being seen to act unethically can cause serious damage to a company's image and the way it is perceived. The majority of companies will operate within the law. However, there are issues that, whilst within the law, may be viewed as unethical by members of the public. For example, advertising alcoholic drinks in such a way that they appear attractive to youngsters is seen as unacceptable by many. Social forces are also particularly significant in terms of tobacco advertising.

Not only are marketers expected to be responsible in the way they structure their campaigns and their message content (so that they are decent and honest), but they must also be ethical in the way they conduct their activities. Advertising to children is forbidden in some countries and the use of children in some advertisements is regulated.

It is very important for products to be promoted in a way that is acceptable to society in general. Therefore, marketers must gauge prevailing opinion and act accordingly. This is a continuing requirement. For example, when there were a number of media reports about sportsmen taking bribes to influence the results of football matches and cricket games, marketers needed to consider if there was any potential risk to their products continuing to be associated through sponsorship with the sport or individuals concerned. The level and nature of risk must also be taken into account before any response is made.

Marketers are expected to act in a socially responsible way, and that may conflict with personal and organisational values and policies. Taking social responsibility means that organisations and marketers need to determine what is right and wrong. When advertising tobacco products, firms must behave ethically, so their future promotions need to be clear about any potential health risks and concentrate on ensuring they only target adults, in a way that enables them to make an informed choice. Threats often open up other opportunities, so there may be an increasing demand for tobacco products that are potentially less harmful and more socially acceptable.

Activity 1.4

Your Manager has asked you to prepare six slides for her to use in a short presentation to the Board about the difference between ethics and social responsibility. Using PowerPoint, or a similar software package, produce the slides.

Relationship marketing

One way in which marketing can be implemented that has developed in recent years is referred to as relationship marketing. This extends the traditional view of marketing, which tended to focus on meeting customer needs, but finished as soon as the purchase transaction was completed.

Relationship marketing has been defined as attracting, maintaining and enhancing customer relationships. This involves not only treating customers differently, but also relating to a wider audience, all with the aim of building relationships with customer markets.

The "Five Markets Model of Relationship Marketing" approach shows the various audiences with which the organisation needs to communicate in order to keep

Marketing Fundamentals

good, profitable customers, that in the long term also provide shareholder value. It is the end customer that provides the profit they are seeking, but if the other "markets" are not looked after on the way, the relationship will suffer.

1. **Influencer** – the government, EU officials, etc.

2. **Employee recruitment markets** – ensuring that the staff who are recruited have the right approach.

3. **Supplier markets** – so that a quality supply of components or materials is available when needed.

4. **Referral markets** – which can be useful sources of new business, for example, legal advisers, insurance advisers, etc.

5. **Internal markets** – ensuring all employees are working together to meet the needs of profitable external customer groups.

In summary, relationship marketing recognises that customers have a long-term value, and looks to take advantage of new technology to develop closer relationships with customers.

Activity 1.5

Imagine you are working for a major car dealership. You have a database of all the customers who have purchased from you in the last three years. List three ways you could use the database to build relationships with your customers.

What legislation impacts on the way in which organisations store, retrieve and use customer data?

Case Study – Virtual reinvention

Procter & Gamble (P&G) are exploiting the many opportunities the Internet provides to improve productivity and offer better value to customers.

The dotcom debacle may be behind us, but how quickly and thoroughly companies seize Internet-based opportunities is fast becoming critical to competitive success. Take just a few current examples from P&G, which is deliberately using the Internet to "reinvent" its marketing and brands along every possible dimension: price, "added value" and relationships.

Two major determinants of price are raw materials and supply chain costs. So P&G is driving down raw materials costs by undertaking "reverse auctions" with suppliers. Its 60 reverse auctions over the last 9 months have yielded a 20% improvement in terms: $100 million off yesterday's $500 million bill.

Indeed, P&G is seeing net-based information as a key source of added value for its brands. One famous example is reflect.com, which sells customised beauty products to individuals over the net. Another is the Pampers Parenting Institute, which provides expert parenting information. Says Chairman John Pepper, 'We have to go beyond our products to provide service and help.'

At the same time P&G is looking to the Internet to drive marketing productivity. Before introducing its new product Crest Whiteners into stores, P&G set up a pre-retail launch web site which attracted 1.2 million visitors and sold 140,000 units (at $44 a throw). Michael Kehoe, General Manager of P&G's global oral care business, estimates this initiative's word-of-mouth effect created 500,000 buyers before any launch advertising or retail distribution began (while earning cash on the way!).

Finally, there's relationship building. P&G is now responding to 45,000 consumer email messages and queries a month. It is also tracking and responding to gossip and rumours about the company and its brands via an Intranet-based "Hoaxbusters" web site.

Now, P&G may not be amazingly special in any individual initiative. Certainly its competitors are doing similar things. But what these examples illustrate is the vast range of opportunities being opened up by the Internet, and the speed with which blue-chip organisations are chasing after them.

Source: Extract from 'Virtual reinvention', *Marketing Business*, July/August 2001.

Questions

1. What categories of "customer value" are identified in the Case Study?

2. How is Procter & Gamble achieving improved "value for money"?

3. Procter & Gamble are building relationships through email contact. Suggest three ways they can ensure this effort does not fail.

SUMMARY OF KEY POINTS

In this Session we have introduced marketing and covered the following key points:

- Marketing has existed for centuries, and can be viewed as an exchange process, a total business concept, and a function within the organisation.
- Customers are looking for more value from the benefits offered to them by a product or service, and the marketer must try to offer more value, or different value than that of their competitors.
- Marketing orientation is difficult to achieve, and involves commitment from senior management and clear communication about the need for a customer focus by everyone in the organisation.
- Companies can attract a negative image if they do not act ethically and in a socially responsible manner.
- Relationship marketing involves developing long-term relationships with customers, and everyone involved in supplying them with your products or services.

Improving and developing own learning

The following projects are designed to help you develop your knowledge and skills further, by carrying out some research yourself. Feedback is not provided for this type of learning because there are no "answers" to be found, but you may wish to discuss your findings with colleagues and fellow students.

Project A

Find out how customer focused your organisation is. Do you have a marketing department? Is there a marketing plan, linked to the corporate plan? Is marketing research carried out regularly? To what extent are all individuals in the organisation working towards customer satisfaction?

> **Project B**
>
> Does your organisation do anything with regard to social responsibility? Is any such activity communicated to the general public? How is this message communicated?

> **Project C**
>
> Look at all the correspondence you receive during a two-week period. Is any of it from a company of which you are a customer? Are they trying to develop a relationship with you? How effective is their communication?

Feedback to activities

Activity 1.1

1. d.
2. c.
3. d.

Activity 1.2

Examples of "value" you could offer might include:

- Value for money – free search for difficult/out of print books.
- Information – catalogues, online catalogues, newsletters or e-newsletters about new books published that month.
- Convenience – offer a choice of method of notification that order is in stock, or offer choice of delivery or collection.

Activity 1.3

This will differ from organisation to organisation. You would be looking for:

1. Continuous research being undertaken.
2. Complaints responded to promptly, recorded, analysed, and action taken.

3. Customer care training carried out, regular communication and briefings to remind and reinforce the message.

Activity 1.4

Slides

1. **Introduction:**
   - Why ethical marketing and social responsibility are important.
   - Increasingly competitive marketplace.
   - Improves company image.

2. **Definition of ethics:**
   Moral philosophies that define right and wrong behaviour in marketing.

3. **Definition of social responsibility:**
   An organisation's responsibility to minimise its negative impact on society as a whole, and maximise its positive impact.

4. **Example of ethical marketing:**
   Researching and satisfying customer needs rather than creating needs.

5. **Example of social responsibility:**
   A large supermarket replanting trees after cutting some down to build a new store.

6. **Conclusion:**
   Adopting an ethical stance and investing money into the local community will help improve corporate image.

Activity 1.5

Three ways in which a database might be used to help build relationships:

1. Analysis of data regarding servicing – reminders sent, possibly with an incentive to use your services.

2. Follow-up call on anniversary of purchase, with discount voucher for valeting or servicing as a "birthday" gift.

3. Analysis of average "re-buy" cycle and proactive contact re new models to encourage return for repurchase.

The Data Protection Act is the legislation that impacts on the way organisations store, retrieve and use customer data.

Session 2

First stages in marketing planning

Introduction

This Session introduces the marketing planning process and the various benefits it offers organisations. It explores the various models that can be used at the analysis stage of the planning process, as well as looking at what an internal and external marketing audit can tell the marketing planner. Finally, it considers the role of marketing research in informing the marketing process.

LEARNING OUTCOMES

At the end of this Session you will be able to:

- Explain the importance of the marketing planning process and the benefits it provides organisations.

- Explain the models that describe the various stages of the marketing planning process.

- Explain the concept of the marketing audit as an appraisal of the external marketing environment and an organisation's internal marketing operations.

- Describe the importance of various analytical tools in the marketing audit process.

- Explain the value of marketing research and information in developing marketing plans.

Marketing planning

The marketing planning process looks at the resources and capabilities of the organisation, identifies and matches them to opportunities presented in the marketplace, and sets out the objectives to be achieved. It then involves the development of a strategy to achieve the objectives, and a detailed plan for implementation and control.

The marketing plan is based on the broader business or corporate plan and clearly outlines what marketing will do to help the organisation meet its corporate objectives.

There are various planning models you will meet as you progress through your marketing studies, and some of these are covered in the next section. The plan serves many purposes, and, if done well, can make the difference between a business's success or failure.

Organisational focus

The marketing plan helps the organisation ensure it stays customer focused. By setting down its objectives, and the processes to be used to achieve them, it is more likely to stay on track. It also helps promote the discipline of monitoring competitor activity and what is going on in the external environment.

Resource allocation

It helps focus marketing management on the resources needed to achieve objectives, and, when budgets are set, provides a means for reviewing them on a regular basis. Resources, of course, are not just financial in nature. The introduction of new physical resources or Information and Communications Technology (ICT) for example, also need to be planned for and justified. The marketing manager also needs to consider how the plan will be resourced in respect of staffing requirements each year. If the plan is more complex and ambitious, will more experienced staff be required or will outside agencies be used?

Responsibilities

As the detailed plan is developed, decisions are made about who will be responsible for each area. The plan provides an ongoing reminder of what tasks are planned, when they will be carried out, and by whom.

Joint effort

The plan also provides a point of focus for all the individuals who are working towards its achievement. Everyone is aware of their individual role, but also knows what goals the team are working towards. The existence of this common goal, and the fact that it provides the individual with a sense of identity, can be motivational.

Management control

The plan assists management to check progress and make adjustments as necessary. Once measurable objectives are set, then regular reviews can be made to check that long-term goals are realistic, given current strategy. It allows

First stages in marketing planning

managers and those involved in implementing the plan to monitor its progress and take action if the organisation falls behind its targets.

Provides "contingency" arrangements

If the external environment is monitored on an ongoing basis, and competitor activity is observed for its likely impact on the organisation's strategy, then the plan can be adjusted to compensate. However, if these eventualities are not anticipated as resources are being allocated, should changes have to be made it may prove difficult or impossible to adjust. Contingencies should be planned for at the same time as the main plan is put together.

Activity 2.1

You have been asked by your local college to make a presentation to the Business Studies class on 'The benefits marketing planning can bring to an organisation'. Prepare six slides for your presentation.

Planning models

There are various planning models or frameworks that can be used when putting together a marketing plan and sub-plans. The one you use will often be based on a structure that is acceptable within your organisation. Generally, they all follow a similar pattern, and the extent to which each stage is sub-divided depends on the particular circumstances in which you are planning. The table overleaf compares some of the most common frameworks used, and shows how the stages of each model link to those in the others.

APIC		SOSTTMMMM	SOSTAC	Marketing Communications Planning Framework
Analysis	Where are we now?	Situation analysis	Situation analysis	Context analysis
Planning	Where do we want to be?	Objectives	Objectives	Promotional objectives
	How might we get there?	Strategy	Strategy	Marketing communications strategy
		Targets		
Implementation	Which way is best?	Tactics	Tactics	Promotional mix (methods, tools and media)
		Men	Action	Resources (human and financial)
		Money		
		Minutes		Schedule and implementation
Control	How can we ensure arrival?	Measurement	Control	Evaluation and control

The stages of the plan are explored further in this Session and in Sessions 3 and 4.

The marketing audit and analytical tools

The marketing audit is a systematic assessment of the organisation's marketing objectives, strategies, organisation and performance. As such, it provides the foundation for setting realistic objectives and defining realistic strategies. It is broadly split into two parts. Firstly, it looks outside the organisation to make sense of the environment the organisation operates in, or might operate in, and identifies opportunities and threats. Secondly, it looks inwardly at how effectively the marketing activities being undertaken are performing, and makes recommendations for the future. Organisations use a marketing audit as a diagnostic exercise – and then take corrective action as necessary.

Like any audit, it should be conducted regularly. Ideally, it should be carried out by someone external to the organisation, to try and get as objective a view as possible.

The audit is made up of the following areas:

a. The marketing environment audit.

b. The marketing strategy audit.

c. The marketing organisation audit.

d. The marketing systems audit.

e. The marketing productivity audit.

f. Marketing function audits.

Let's look at each of these components in turn.

The marketing environment audit

This is an audit of all the factors outside an organisation which have an impact on the way it does its marketing. These factors are outside of the control of the organisation, so they must adjust their marketing plan, or build their marketing plan accordingly.

The audit is most commonly referred to as a PEST analysis – Political, Economic, Social and Technological factors.

Political – what laws affect our marketing practice? Is the law likely to change? Is the government likely to change, and is this likely to affect our business?

Economic – will the levels of inflation or unemployment affect our business? Will interest rates go up or down? How would this affect us?

Social – are consumer lifestyles changing, and do we need to respond to this? From an ecological standpoint, how will our packaging and processes be viewed by the public?

Technological – what changes are taking place from a technological perspective? Will our competitors have an advantage over us through new technology?

It also looks at the influences on the company's micro-environment – the markets within which the company operates. It considers such questions as "What is happening to our market – is it growing or shrinking?" and "Which segments offer the best opportunities for us in the future?" It also looks at customers, competitors, distributors and channels of distribution, suppliers, and other publics – considering the potential changes that might affect them and therefore your organisation. This can be a complex and detailed part of the marketing audit and, at this level, you need only be aware that it is taking place. You may be asked to take part in this part of the audit in your organisation, but you should be given appropriate guidance. It is covered in more detail in the higher levels of the qualifications.

The marketing strategy audit

This part of the audit looks at the business mission, marketing objectives, and marketing strategy. Is everything clear? Are we still focused and heading in the right direction?

The marketing organisation audit

How is the marketing function structured, and is it appropriate to ensure customer focus? Are there good relationships between the marketing department and the other functions? Are we well resourced, and do the changes we are making mean that staff training is necessary?

First stages in marketing planning

The marketing systems audit

This section of the audit looks at the organisation's marketing information system, the marketing planning system, the marketing control system and the new product development system and processes. Are they still effective for our purposes?

The marketing productivity audit

This considers the relative cost-effectiveness of the marketing activities against results, and whether any changes need to be made. It also looks at the profitability of each product, each segment that is targeted, each channel of distribution and each market. In doing so, it will help inform decisions about future strategy.

Marketing function audits

Finally, the audit looks at each element of the marketing mix in detail, and, where appropriate, looks at the size, composition and effectiveness of the sales force.

The marketing audit feeds information into a **SWOT** analysis. The analysis of the organisation and its resources and capabilities reveals **Strengths** and **Weaknesses**, whilst the PEST and micro-environmental analyses reveal **Opportunities** and **Threats**. The SWOT analysis allows the marketer to make recommendations to feed into the marketing strategy.

The SWOT and PEST analyses are just two of the tools that organisations can use in the analysis stage of the planning process. The function of these tools is to help structure the search for, and analysis of, information, to arrive at a meaningful and comprehensive picture of the organisation and its environment.

Activity 2.2

What are the elements of the following frameworks? Give an example of each one for your own organisation.

1. PEST.
2. SWOT.

Marketing research and its role in planning

If an organisation is to meet and anticipate its customer needs, then it needs to find out what they are, and keep track of ways in which they may be changing. It is not appropriate or wise to make assumptions, and those companies that have made the mistake of doing so have found the experience very costly.

Marketing research is an essential part of the planning process, and covers not only customer research, but also product research, promotional research, distribution research and sales research. All of the information gathered, together with information gathered about the marketing environment, is fed into a marketing information system. This is covered in much more detail in the Marketing Environment module.

The marketing planning process is about carrying out analysis in many forms, as the marketing audit section highlights, and then making a series of decisions based on the analysis undertaken. It needs to answer such questions as:

- What opportunities and threats does the external environment offer us?
- Are these the same as last year, and how are they likely to change?
- What are our internal strengths, and what resources do we have available to us?
- What do our customers want, and how is this changing?
- What new options are available to us to enable us to grow?
- What products and services do we need to develop, and in the light of this knowledge, which are no longer selling?
- What prices should we charge?
- Which channels should we use to get our products to market?
- What promotional tools will be the best ones to use?
- Which media are most appropriate?
- How will we measure the effectiveness of these activities?

Marketing research is the process for gathering information that is not already available to marketers to help them make these decisions. Marketing research is broken down into **quantitative** research (which can be analysed statistically and the results expressed numerically) and **qualitative** research (which deals with opinions or value judgements).

First stages in marketing planning

In gathering marketing research, marketers have two forms of data available to them.

Primary research – information gathered for a specific purpose, either through observation or survey.

Secondary research – information gathered for a purpose other than the specific research objective being pursued.

Both of these types of data have their strengths and weaknesses, and these are covered in more depth in the Marketing Environment module.

Activity 2.3

Explain what secondary research is, and why it is often important to conduct secondary research before primary research.

Case Study – Legal eagles

Davies Lavery, recently awarded Law Firm of the Year at the Insurance Industry Awards, is a 13-year-old insurance law firm, employing 120 people across its three offices in London, Maidstone and Birmingham. Its expertise is in defence for corporations involved in everything from personal injury to conveyancing and employment law.

Two years ago, Davies Lavery's sole marketing activity was an ad hoc programme of corporate hospitality and a not very impressive company brochure. However, research led to a strategic business plan that clearly demonstrated the need for focused, effective marketing. In 1999, the firm hired Chartered Marketer Paula Allerton, who had ten years of business-to-business marketing experience, and who was then Marketing Services Manager for Lloyd's of London. She says 'Obviously a key element of working with a professional services firm is the fact that you are dealing with a partnership where everyone wants a say, and where decisions are often made by committee. This can be frustrating and, as a marketer, you need to understand how each person ticks and deal with them accordingly.'

Allerton put together a focused one-year marketing plan for Davies Lavery, which revolved around presenting a professional image, whilst maintaining factors that she felt made the firm special, such as its excellent client relationships.

She wanted a positive image that showed the firm to be forward-looking and no-nonsense, and to create this she determined on a new corporate identity to encapsulate these values, in a style that would run across internal and external communications.

She employed a design company to redesign the logo and develop a corporate ID and "house-style", whilst she wrote a press campaign (both advertising and editorial) for directories, specialist magazines and local newspapers.

In addition, she got a publishing company to create and publish a quarterly newsletter to give clients and prospects information in a concise, "non-techy" way. To overcome the perennial problem of "information overload", Allerton demanded short, factual articles, conveying only essential information, but with links to further source material for those people with a particular interest.

The hub of all Davies Lavery's marketing activity is its new web site, which is regularly maintained and is becoming a useful tool for clients. Allerton has also created an e-newsletter that goes to clients and prospects on a monthly basis.

Like many law firms, Davies Lavery now enjoys the benefits of a comprehensive, accurate, and regularly cleaned database, as well as a programme to raise the profile of its partners, who now regularly speak at key events. In addition, teams in all disciplines have consistent, professional sales packs, that convey the corporate ID and which are specifically designed to cross-sell the firm's skills.

Eighteen months down the line, Davies Lavery has retained its core values while enjoying a ten-fold increase in editorial coverage. Its commitment to marketing has turned its 1998 vision to be a 'premier niche insurance law firm' into a reality.

Source: Extract from 'Legal eagles', *Marketing Business*, March 2001.

Questions

1. How is the organisation described before it had a marketing plan in place?

2. What specific actions can you identify that were taken as a result of the plan being in place?

3. What results of the plan can you identify?

SUMMARY OF KEY POINTS

In this Session we have explored the role of marketing planning, and covered the following key points:

- The marketing planning process plays an important role in focusing the organisation on the customer.
- It also helps give individuals in the marketing department a common goal to work towards.
- There are several planning frameworks, all of which go through four main phases – analysis, planning, implementation and control.
- The marketing audit is a thorough analysis of all aspects of marketing, as well as of external influences on the organisation.
- Marketing research gathers valuable data that can contribute to the decision-making process about the direction of the plan.

Improving and developing own learning

The following projects are designed to help you develop your knowledge and skills further, by carrying out some research yourself. Feedback is not provided for this type of learning because there are no "answers" to be found, but you may wish to discuss your findings with colleagues and fellow students.

Marketing Fundamentals

> **Project A**
>
> Carry out a SWOT analysis on your own organisation, or one you know well.

> **Project B**
>
> Carry out a PEST analysis for your own organisation, or one you know well.

> **Project C**
>
> Find out which planning framework is used by your own marketing department. Link the stages to those shown in the table. What analytical models are used as part of the marketing audit?

Feedback to activities

Activity 2.1

Slides

1. **Introduction:**

    Importance of planning.

2. **Helps to give the organisation direction:**
    - Helps focus activity.
    - Ensures external environment is scanned regularly.
    - Monitors competitor activity and researches customer needs.

3. **Helps ensure resources are allocated appropriately:**
    - Ensures that sufficient budget is invested.
    - Ensures that sufficient numbers of employees are involved in customer-focused activity.
    - Ensures that appropriate systems are put in place.

First stages in marketing planning

4. **Ensures staff recognise their responsibilities:**
   - Employees take responsibility for parts of the plan being implemented.
   - Staff "pull together" to ensure that the goals are met.
   - Employees are aware of a common goal and work together to achieve it.

5. **Control mechanisms are put in place:**
   - Ensures activity is monitored for effectiveness.
   - Regular reviews are carried out.
   - Identifies reasons for non-achievement.
   - Corrective action can be taken.

6. **Changing environment:**
   - Provides processes to anticipate changes in the environment that will impact on activity.
   - Enables allowances to be made for contingencies.

Activity 2.2

Examples will differ depending on your organisation. You should have identified one example for each of the following categories:

1. Political.
   Economic.
   Social.
   Technological.

2. Strengths.
   Weaknesses.
   Opportunities.
   Threats.

Activity 2.3

Secondary research – research carried out for another purpose than the current research objective.

It is often considered before primary research is carried out, as it is already available and can therefore save both time and money.

41

Session 3

The marketing plan

Introduction

This Session looks at how the analysis covered in Session 2 is used within the marketing plan, and how it links together with the other phases of the remainder of the plan. It looks at the importance of setting SMART objectives in planning, and how this simplifies the evaluation/control phase of the plan. It also looks at the role of segmentation in both consumer and business-to-business markets as the foundation of a marketing strategy, and how management structures can affect the success of the plan.

LEARNING OUTCOMES

At the end of this Session you will be able to:

- Explain the importance of objectives, and the influences on, and processes for, setting objectives.
- Explain the concept of market segmentation, and distinguish effective bases for segmenting consumer and business-to-business markets.
- Describe the structure of an outline marketing plan and identify its various components.
- Depict the various management structures available for implementing marketing plans, and understand their advantages and disadvantages.
- Examine the factors that affect the setting of marketing budgets.
- Demonstrate an appreciation of the need to monitor and control marketing activities.

Marketing objectives

The setting of marketing objectives is an important part of the marketing planning process. Unless we know what we are aiming to achieve, we are unlikely to achieve it! Marketing objectives should be closely linked to the organisation's objectives. Indeed, they represent what marketing is looking to achieve – to help the organisation meet its objectives.

All objectives should be SMART. That is:

Specific.
Measurable.
Achievable.
Relevant.
Time-bound.

For example, compare the following two objectives.

1. To make more profit than last year, by selling our products in Germany as well as the UK.

2. To increase sales of air fresheners by 10% of last year's figures, by 31st March 2003.

The first of these is confusing. It is partly objective and partly strategy (i.e. it not only looks at **what** we want to achieve, it also looks at **how** we are going to do it).

The second is **S**pecific (about the sales volume of air fresheners), **M**easurable (an increase of 10%), **A**chievable (we cannot tell without knowing what was sold last year, but we can assume that whoever set the objective has this knowledge), **R**elevant (again, we have to assume that it links to the company's objectives), and **T**ime-bound (it must be achieved by 31st March 2003).

Influences on marketing objectives

Corporate objectives

The key influence on marketing objectives is that of corporate objectives. The marketing plan may have several objectives, each of which must relate to the organisation's objectives. For example, if the company is looking to grow, then the marketing objective may be concerned with growing market share, entering new markets or targeting new segments. If the organisation is looking to make more profit, then the marketing objective may also be concerned with marketing for profitability. They may also concern customer satisfaction or brand awareness, but the key issue here is that they stay **relevant**.

Organisation resources

Objectives must be **achievable**, and if you do not have the budget, or the human resources to carry out your plan, then it will not be achieved. You must work within the constraints presented by the size of your organisation and its financial and management stability.

Time span

Objectives must be **time-bound**, so if your plan is a one-year marketing plan, objectives that will be met within eighteen months will not be **relevant**. Scale down what you are looking to achieve by setting "milestones" of what is possible within a twelve-month period. Remember also that if you do not review a twelve-month objective until the end of the period, it will be too late to make any adjustments to your plan. You should set interim review dates.

Outcomes of analysis undertaken

The analysis you have undertaken within the marketing audit, specifically your PEST analysis, will have given you a picture of external influences on your marketing objectives. Objectives must be written with these external, non-controllable factors in mind, or they will not be **achievable**.

Culture and leadership

Organisational culture and leadership will also influence the way your marketing objectives are set. For example, an organisation with a cautious leadership style may have the prime objectives of remaining stable within the marketplace, and minimising risk. **Relevant** marketing objectives for this culture may have an emphasis on price and service standards, to maintain their position in the marketplace.

Nature of the market

The degree to which the market is growing, or contracting, will also impact upon the marketing objectives set. It may not be realistic (or **achievable**) to set a marketing objective to grow your market share by 30%, if your products are in decline and the market is contracting!

How marketing objectives are set

Corporate objectives are set by senior management who have envisioned where the organisation will be in a number of years time. Marketing objectives represent what marketing is looking to achieve to help the organisation meet those objectives.

The key information from your marketing audit is summarised in the SWOT analysis. From this information you will be able to identify what products or services customers want, and why they want them, and from your competitor analysis you can see what your competitors are doing. Therefore you can determine which segments will be the best to target. You will also have analysed the performance of each of your products, in terms of their life cycle and profitability. In summary, this information gives you a snapshot of where your organisation is now.

Within the constraints of your organisation's resources, and the influences set out above, you will now be in a position to start to develop the marketing objectives that can bridge the gap between where the organisation is now and where it wants to be in the future.

Marketing objectives are normally set by managers, and then approved by the senior management team.

Once they are approved, then sub-objectives will be set in terms of communications objectives, sales objectives, public relations objectives, etc.

Activity 3.1

Write SMART objectives for each of the following scenarios:

1. Harrop's Shoes make the finest leather shoes for ladies. The Managing Director wants the company to grow, and has decided that the company will produce copies of their successful range for younger women next year.

2. Mapp's Computer Services set up only two years ago, and has so far done very well repairing home computers for customers in their local town. This year a competitor has set up nearby, and Gerry Mapp has decided that the only way he can continue to increase his profit level by 10% per year is to start to offer repair services to local companies as well.

You should make up any information you do not have.

Market segmentation

One option open to companies, particularly those who are operating in very competitive markets, is to segment the market into smaller groups, and then target specific segments more effectively. Small companies often have only a few customers, whom they know well, and treat them individually. Larger companies with many more customers cannot realistically treat every customer individually, so it makes sense to group customers in some way that enables the company to treat each group the same. This is what marketers call segmentation.

Segmentation involves dividing the market into smaller, more similar, targetable groups. These similarities mean that organisations can choose the most suitable to target (depending on the resources they have available, the competitive situation, and their own organisational objectives). When they have decided which segment they wish to target, they can devise a marketing mix to suit the specific needs and buying behaviour of that group of customers.

Segmentation will only be effective if segments can be seen to meet the following criteria:

Measurable – can we measure the number of people or firms within a segment, or their total purchasing power, or their potential for profit?

Accessible – how easily can we reach the customers within the segment? It may be necessary to combine geographical segmentation with another method to make a segment accessible.

Substantial – will the segment be large or profitable enough to deserve a special marketing mix?

Actionable – have we got the resources to target the number of segments we have identified? If not, we may have to re-segment, identifying larger segments with not quite so separate needs.

Segmentation can be approached in a number of different ways and is likely to be done differently in consumer, or business-to-consumer (b2c) markets, than in business-to-business (b2b) markets.

Consumer segmentation

Consumer markets can be segmented by many variables, as shown below.

Demographics – age, sex, family, race, religion, family life cycle.

Socio-economics – income, occupation, education, social class.

Geography – country, region, type of housing.

Personality, motives and lifestyle – psychographics is one of the main methods of lifestyle segmentation, and looks at peoples' attitudes, opinions and interests.

Purchase behaviour – loyal to a well-known brand, look for cheapest price, look for something new.

Purchase occasion – emergency purchase versus purchase through choice.

Benefits sought – segmenting by the benefits potential purchasers are looking for.

User status – heavy purchasers versus light purchasers, users versus non-users.

Attitude towards product – for example, clothing. Some buyers want designer labels, some want quality and style, others want hard wearing and practical.

The following table contrasts Air Swiss, which is known for its comfort and reliability, and easyJet, who offer low prices and convenient booking arrangements. Contrasting segments for Air Swiss and easyJet might therefore be identified through a combination of socio-economic and demographic variables, and customer benefits sought.

Variable	Air Swiss	easyJet
Age	35+	18-35
Income	Middle to high income bands – disposable income may be higher because home is established.	Low to middle income bands. May still be students. Disposable income may be lower as trying to establish home.
Stage in family life cycle	Established "couples" or career "singles". May have young family.	Young singles or couples.

Variable	Air Swiss	easyJet
Benefits sought		
Comfort	✓	
Reliability	✓	
Convenience		✓
Low prices		✓

Business-to-business segmentation

Segmentation can also be applied to business-to-business markets (previously referred to as industrial segmentation), although different criteria are used. The most commonly used criteria are:

Type of industry/industry demographics – industry type (SIC code), size, location.

Situational factors – those needing quick delivery versus those needing standard delivery terms, or how they use the product or service, or whether they are large purchasers or small.

Type of buying structure – type of Decision Making Unit (DMU), centralised versus decentralised purchasing, preferred supplier basis.

The marketing plan

The role of the marketing plan was covered in the previous Session, as was the analysis stage. The full marketing plan involves the following stages.

Situation analysis:

- Of the organisation's environment and trends – Political, Economic, Sociological and Technological (PEST). Technology is particularly important for Internet companies for example, as they need to keep up with developments in order to retain customers and compete.

- Of customer needs and wants. For example, who is using the Internet? How do they access it? When and where from? Which groups do we want to target, and what do they want from us?

- Of competitor activity. For Internet companies this is relatively easy to monitor because of the nature of the Internet. Once you know who they are, it is difficult to predict which new competitors will come onto the scene, as the Internet has low "entry barriers" for other new start-ups.

- Of channels to market. What channels are available to reach the desired markets? What are the characteristics of each? Are there any opportunities to serve new segments or markets by setting up a new channel?

- Of the organisation's strengths, weaknesses, opportunities and threats. Internet companies have been under threat through pressure from their investors to return a profit or be closed down. They therefore need to carefully manage their growth.

Objectives:

- Marketing objectives should be Specific, Measurable, Achievable, Relevant and Time-bound (SMART). An example for an Internet company might be 'to establish ourselves as the market leading web media company by the end of December 2003.'

Strategy:

- Identifying and selecting target segments.
- Specifying a basis for establishing competitive advantage.
- Basis for establishing growth – for example, Ansoff's matrix may help us to determine a general direction from which to achieve growth.

The Ansoff Matrix provides a link between products and markets by considering the combination shown in the diagram opposite, giving four potential strategies for growth for a UK producer of indigestion tablets for example.

Ansoff's product/market matrix

	Product: Current	Product: New
Market: Current	Market penetration* More sales of antacid product to existing customers – UK.	Product development** Develop product, adding fruit flavours for sale through pharmacists.
Market: New	Market development** Extend sales to France and Germany.	Diversification*** Calcium in product means new product can be developed for treatment of osteoporosis.

Source: Adapted from Ansoff.

The number of asterisks* shown against each strategy indicates the differing levels of risk involved in adopting it.

Market penetration – growth is achieved by increasing sales of existing products in existing markets. Heavy promotion may help achieve this. It is low risk because the customer is already a "known".

Product development – companies develop new products in order to grow. New product development carries a risk of failure. However, by managing the product portfolio carefully and having existing products that can support the new ones the risk is reduced.

Market development – this strategy involves companies looking for new markets for their products. This can be geographical, or could be the repositioning of a product to attract a new market.

Diversification – this involves companies moving into areas that they have not previously been involved in, both new products and new markets. This obviously carries the highest risk, as both are unfamiliar.

Marketing Fundamentals

Detailed plan (the marketing mix):
- Product.
- Price.
- Promotion.
- Place.
- People.
- Process.
- Physical evidence.

This details who will be responsible for what, and what financial resources are necessary.

Control:
- How progress on the objectives will be monitored.
- How often reviews of each part of the plan will be undertaken.
- Who is responsible for reviewing and adjusting the plan?

Activity 3.2

Identify and explain three possible ways of segmenting the market for:

1. Shoes.
2. Ice cream.
3. A4 paper.

Management structures, and how they affect the implementation of the plan

Marketing plans have to be put into practice before any results will be seen. This is a complex process, and there are many barriers that can get in the way of its successful implementation. In Session 1, when we talked about marketing as a total business philosophy, we identified the need for senior management support to achieve a marketing orientation. The way an organisation and its marketing division are organised can impact on how well marketing is implemented.

First let's look at a typical organisational structure for a medium-sized manufacturer.

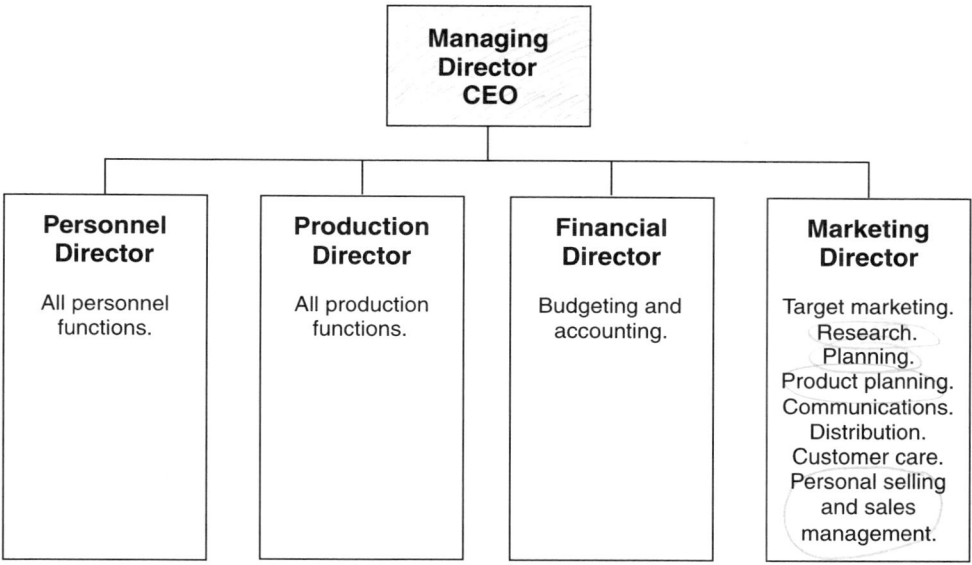

The above structure is ideal for the achievement of a customer-focused organisation. The Marketing Director is on the same level as other senior managers, and has total responsibility for all marketing-related functions.

However, it is not just a case of restructuring, as we discussed in the first Session. A true marketing orientation can only come from a structure and culture that enables a customer-focused culture.

Now let's consider the options for structuring the marketing function.

Marketing teams are commonly organised by product, by customer group, by activity or by geographical area. Organisations have to decide which structure is most suitable for effective implementation of their own marketing plan and overall circumstances.

Product – where an organisation is offering a complex or diverse range of products it is appropriate to organise the marketing structure around particular products or product groups. In this case the Marketing Manager is often referred to as a Product Manager.

Customer group – this structure is most appropriate where the segments targeted vary greatly. For example, a stationery and consumables producer may sell direct to large companies, as well as to large retailers such as Office World or Staples. The needs of the two groups may demand different marketing mixes, and so separate Marketing Managers may have responsibility for each.

Activity/function – this centralised structure is adopted by some large companies whose customers are very similar. The structure may involve a Marketing Research Manager, a Product Development Manager, an Advertising Manager, and a Sales Manager, all reporting to the Marketing Director.

Geography – this structure may be most appropriate for organisations that operate internationally, or whose customer groups differ from one area to another. The structure has a full marketing team for each region.

Activity 3.3

1. Talk to staff in your Marketing Department and find out how it is structured. Which Director is responsible for marketing? What does that tell you about the importance of marketing in the company and the strength of its marketing orientation?

2. Draw the structure.

3. Identify which of the descriptions above matches your organisation most appropriately, and write a few notes justifying the structure used.

Factors affecting the setting of marketing budgets

The methods used by companies to set their marketing or communications budgets differ greatly, and are influenced by the culture of the company and the resources it has available. Some are very subjective and based on one individual's judgement. Others are based on the objective that is to be achieved, which then avoids the risk of judging wrongly and wasting the money spent.

Objective and task

This method focuses on what goals are to be achieved and then decides how much it will be necessary to spend to achieve them. An organisation with a strong marketing orientation will often use this approach.

Competitor based/competitor parity

This method involves finding out what your competitors are spending. A decision is then made about how much you need to spend to compete – this may be equal (parity), or proportionate, depending on relative market share held and marketing objectives set.

All we can afford

This method relies on one (usually senior) person in the organisation making a decision about what will be available to spend, and communicating this to all concerned. This method is often used by smaller, newer companies.

Percentage of sales

This is a commonly used technique and, when calculated on last year's sales, is not very effective. Imagine having an objective to increase sales volume with a budget based on what was achieved last year! This method lacks a forward view and does not take into account any changes in the marketing environment or changes in media prices. An organisation may make the decision to allocate say 10% of their sales to marketing for the next year. They will then base the percentage figure around the known "norm" for their industry. The negatives of this method are that by basing their spend on what they achieved last year, the company are limiting the amount of marketing activity they can undertake to a lower amount. A slightly more effective approach is based on predicted sales for the coming year.

Same as Last Time (SALT)

This method speaks for itself. However, it is again not very forward looking and does not even carry an increase to allow for inflation.

Planned marketing activity should drive demand for your products or services. If you limit the amount you invest, then you are limiting the demand you create.

In summary, factors that affect the budget set for marketing plans include:

- The marketing objectives to be achieved.
- The resources available.
- The culture of the organisation.
- The method of budget setting adopted.

The importance of monitoring and controlling the plan

The final stage in the marketing planning process, control, aims to build-in mechanisms that regularly review the progress of the plan. There are three main stages involved in any review process.

1. Setting measurable standards of performance.
2. Evaluating performance against these standards as the organisation implements the plan.
3. Making any adjustments necessary to the plan as variances occur.

The measurable standards for performance have been set in the form of SMART objectives. When evaluating performance to objectives you need to consider what has happened, how this compares to the objectives, how any variances might be explained, and what action needs to be taken.

Unless progress to the plan is reviewed on a regular basis, then it may be too late to adjust it to keep on track to achieve the objectives. What happens in the external environment can impact on performance against the plan. For example, an unexpected rise in interest rates may mean that customers order in smaller quantities, slowing progress. An early adjustment to price, or the level of personal selling activity in trying to attract new customers may compensate, but if it is left to the end of the year it will be too late to take any action.

This stage of the plan is covered in more depth in Session 10.

Activity 3.4

Moors Duvets spent £375,000 on its marketing activity last year. This resulted in sales of £5 million. Their marketing objective for this year is 'To achieve a 10% increase in sales value on duvet sales by the end of 2003'. Their largest competitor is thought to have budgeted £400,000, and has increased their market share from 18% to 20% of the market in the last year. Moors has a 25% market share.

1. Calculate the marketing budget on a same as last time (SALT) basis.
2. Calculate the marketing budget on the basis of the planned 10% increase in sales.
3. Calculate the marketing budget on a competitor basis.

Case Study – Never too old

Martin Smith offers some advice to marketers on the process of targeting the lucrative over-50s market.

Professor Germaine Greer is annoyed. Apparently no one is trying to sell her anything. Unbelievable as this may seem, Greer assured those present at the International Advertising Association (IAA) Congress in June, that marketers were avoiding her for the simple fact that she is 61 years old. By raising this point in a discussion on the issue of gender and advertising, Greer touched on a subject that despite its enormity and obviousness is still being ignored by advertisers – the growth of the mature market.

The fact that we're living longer means that the so-called "grey market" is currently the fastest growing demographic sector in Europe. But many of these consumers do not feel old and do not want to be treated as such. As Jack Nicholson said on turning 61, 'Our generation are the new old. I remember what someone of 60 looked like when I was a kid. They didn't look like me.'

In many respects, the 50-year-old consumer has the same basic desires as the 20-year-old. They both want to live safely, comfortably, healthily and pleasurably. However, what is important to one 20-year-old does not automatically apply to all 20-year-olds, and a marketer would be foolish to make this assumption. The same is true of consumers over 50, yet many marketing strategies still group several different age and lifestyle categories together when targeting this market. Like any other superficial demarcation of consumer groups, men, women, teenagers, mothers, etc., the mature sector is complex and needs to be approached and targeted with the same degree of segmentation as any other market.

Basic segmentation

Because of the size and complexity of the mature market, some rudimentary age band segmentation should be undertaken to begin to understand it. In very simple terms, the market can be divided into the three age bands below.

- **Thrivers** (aged 50-59) experienced their formative years through the teenage rebellion of the 1960s. They are now the most affluent, active and healthy of any people this age throughout history.
- **Seniors** (aged 60-69 years) spent their formative years coping with rationing and living frugally. These experiences and attitudes often remain with them. They are generally not interested in instant gratification but concern themselves with health issues and personal comfort.
- **Elders** (those over 70) grew up in a time of great hardship. In general the "make do and mend" attitude is still evident. Because of this they are generally free of debt and intend to stay that way.

However, these categories only provide a very basic insight into this audience. They are generalisations. As with younger markets, it is essential to focus and segment according to income, lifestyle and life stages, to create a more rounded picture.

Targeting your market

The design of material aimed at older consumers is important. Considerations such as deteriorating eyesight should influence planning. For example, layouts need to be uncluttered and soft colours and small typefaces should also be avoided.

Imagery that appeals to younger markets is likely to alienate older consumers who will not take the time to understand a message if it is not immediately obvious. An image that is used repeatedly in marketing aimed at older consumers is that of a sunset – despite its complete lack of appeal to the intended market! If you must use the sun, why not try a sunrise instead?

The marketing plan

Naturally, the choice of words and phrasing has to match the target audience, using a language that is familiar. Although it is obvious to avoid jargon, other things that will alienate are not always so clear. For example, a company targeting the mature sector is likely to irritate its audience if it begins sentences with "and" or "but".

The choice of medium available for reaching this age group is as wide as for any other market – including the Internet. This sector watches more television than any other group and is steadily beginning to spend more time online. Vavo.com and lifebegins.net are just two of a growing number of sites devoted to the over-50s.

However, the most effective method of targeting the senior market remains direct mail. Many older consumers can feel isolated because of their age and warm to companies that address them personally in a familiar medium. Establishing and developing a relationship with mature customers is vital, so careful targeting of initial communications is important. Likewise, they appreciate and expect a high level of customer care, so any marketing strategy needs to be backed by a good Customer Relationship Management (CRM) programme.

Because so few companies have concentrated on targeting this lucrative market, it is still wide open. The "50 plussers" are the market that spends the most on cars, they are the people buying sports cars, and they own more off-road vehicles than any other group in society. They also spend the most on holidays, financial products, and they dominate the market for luxury goods. Why not capitalise on this audience now and leave the short-sighted and trendy to the waning youth market?

Martin Smith is Managing Director of Millennium Direct.

Source: 'Never Too Old', *Marketing Business*, September 2000.

Questions

1. What are the three segments identified in the Case Study?

2. Which segment might be best to target for a new design of open top, high-performance car?

3. Identify three examples of approaches to communication that the Case Study highlights as being relevant to these segments.

SUMMARY OF KEY POINTS

In this Session we have looked at the planning, implementation and control aspects of the marketing plan and covered the following key points:

- Markets can be segmented so that more effective marketing mixes can be designed.
- There are various approaches to segmenting both consumer and business-to-business markets.
- The marketing plan follows a step-by-step design:
  - Situation analysis.
  - Objective setting.
  - Strategy.
  - Targets.
  - Tactics – 7 Ps.
  - Action – who is responsible, what financial resources are required, when will tactics be undertaken.
  - Control – review and evaluation measures.
- The structure of the organisation and the marketing department can impact on the implementation of marketing plans.
- There are several ways of allocating marketing budgets.
- The evaluation of progress against the plan is a very important stage if objectives are to be met in a changing environment.

Improving and developing own learning

The following projects are designed to help you develop your knowledge and skills further, by carrying out some research yourself. Feedback is not provided for this type of learning because there are no "answers" to be found, but you may wish to discuss your findings with colleagues and fellow students.

The marketing plan

Project A
Look at the web site of any major car manufacturer and try to identify the profile of the segment being targeted by each model in their range.

Project B
Find out how the market for your products or services is segmented, and make notes about how the segments differ for each product in the range. Can you identify any other ways the market could be segmented?

Project C
Talk to your Marketing Manager to discover how the budget for marketing is set each year.

Feedback to activities

Activity 3.1

There are no right or wrong answers here, but you should check the objectives you have written against the SMART criteria in the text (make sure you have not included "strategy" in your objective).

1. To achieve a 15% increase in sales of ladies shoes by the end of March 2004.

2. To achieve an increase of 10% in profits for computer servicing by the end of December 2003.

Activity 3.2

1. Children's hard-wearing school shoes – demographics.
   Running shoes – lifestyle.
   Ladies' shoes – demographics.

2. Sophisticated dessert – situational.
   Child's ice lolly – demographics.
   Catering pack – business-to-business.

Marketing Fundamentals

3. Business-to-business purchase:
   - To discount "sheds" such as Office World.
   - Direct to small businesses for printing.
   - In bulk to businesses with more than 200 employees for printing and photocopying.

Activity 3.3
Your answer to this will depend on your own organisation, but you should check what you have found by rereading the text and checking against the essential reading.

Activity 3.4
1. £375,000.
2. £412,500.
3. £500,000.

Session 4

The marketing mix

Introduction

Having looked at how markets are segmented in the previous Session, this Session considers how specific segments are selected and targeted with a marketing mix created to meet the needs of each segment. More detailed coverage of each element of the marketing mix can be found in Sessions 5-9.

> **LEARNING OUTCOMES**
>
> At the end of this Session you will be able to:
>
> - Describe the essential elements of targeting and positioning, and the creation of an integrated and coherent marketing mix.
>
> - Describe the wide range of tools and techniques available to marketers to satisfy customer requirements and compete effectively.
>
> - Explain the development of the extended marketing mix concept to include additional components in appropriate contextual settings: product, price, place (distribution), promotion (communication), people, processes, physical evidence and customer service.

Targeting and positioning

Segmentation, targeting and positioning is a process by which customers can be categorised into groups with similar needs, characteristics and buying habits, and can then be targeted with products and services relevant to their needs. This enables companies to "target" a group of customers with the same marketing mix, saving time and money.

The marketing mix

The full process goes through three stages:

When a number of segments have been identified, the company can decide which, if any, they should target. There are three main options open to companies in terms of market coverage:

1. **Undifferentiated marketing**

    This means that the company has decided to focus on the characteristics that all its customers share, rather than dividing the market into segments. A common marketing mix is then developed and used to target all potential customers. The methods used by this type of company are referred to as mass production, mass communication and mass distribution. This method is what Henry Ford was describing when he made his famous quote 'Customers can have any colour so long as it's black.'

2. **Differentiated marketing**

   With this option the company decides to target a number of segments, each with a slightly different marketing mix. Car manufacturers provide a good example of the use of this type of strategy.

3. **Concentrated marketing**

   This option involves the company selecting one, or a very small number of segments. It focuses very specifically on the customers' needs, and tries to meet them in a more effective way than their competitors do. It is often used with high-quality goods such as Rolex watches, or Rolls-Royce cars.

The criteria for ensuring that a segment will be effective were covered in the last Session. This process is often used by smaller companies to help them identify a niche in the market that larger companies have not catered for, and so define a basis for competing with larger players. They may consider developing new products for a segment that has not been specifically targeted. For example, banks have identified a segment they call the "mass affluent", who are alike in terms of the amount they earn and so have money available to invest. They are developing new investment products through the Internet to meet their needs, with the aim of attracting them from their current banks.

When looking at the marketing planning process, segmentation and targeting can play an important part as, linked with strategy, they can help the company decide how they are going to meet their marketing objectives, and how they can develop the most appropriate marketing mix.

Activity 4.1

Consider the possible target markets for ballpoint pens, from the value end of the range, to the solid gold exclusive end of the range. Write a brief description of the profile of the group of customers for:

1. The cheap, "plastic tube" type of ballpoint pen.

2. The type of ballpoint pen that might be given as a gift.

3. The solid gold, exclusive ballpoint pen.

The marketing mix

The marketing mix, or 4 Ps, is a framework that helps the marketing manager make decisions about what emphasis to place on marketing activity in each area. The marketing mix should be created to best satisfy the needs of a target segment of customers.

The marketing mix is made up of four main components.

Product – the product mix is covered in more depth in Session 5. It involves decisions about developments of new products, which products to stop offering, and product modifications to keep pace with changing customer needs as well as changes in the external environment.

Price – the price mix is covered in more depth in Session 6. It involves decisions on pricing policy, methods and tactics. It links pricing of products to the required positioning of the product in the mind of the consumer, and ensures the price suggests an appropriate quality image for the product or service.

Place – the place mix is covered in more depth in Session 7. It involves decisions about the costs of getting products to the consumer, and the options to do so. It covers such issues as the selection of intermediaries and developing storage and transport systems.

Promotion – the promotional mix is covered in more depth in Session 8. It involves decisions about which promotional tools are most appropriate, what message is suitable for the audience, co-ordinating the tools so that a consistent message is communicated, and which media to use.

Returning to our banking example and the "mass affluent" segment, considerations may be as follows:

Product – should new investment products be developed for the Internet and the mass affluent segment?

Price – Internet services cost us less to deliver than over the counter advice. Will we be able to service sufficient customers over the Internet, at the cheaper rate, to enable us to give advice to those who prefer a "bricks and mortar" service? Will we make a profit without increasing fees (prices)?

Promotion – which publications do this segment read? What do they watch on TV? Which is the best medium to use to target our message at them? How should the message be phrased?

Place – do we make this an "Internet-only" facility or do we need "bricks and mortar" support?

Activity 4.2

A medium-sized furniture manufacturer is looking to move from the provision of basic home furnishings to designing and producing durable office furniture on a business-to-business basis. Complete the following table, contrasting the marketing mix for the existing consumer market and the proposed business-to-business market. Use a spreadsheet to reproduce the table.

	Home furnishings	**Office furnishings**
Product		
Price		
Place		
Promotion		

The extended marketing mix

The extended marketing mix for services consists of the four elements covered above, plus a further three elements, which are designed to deal with the fact that services are different to products. These elements are covered in more depth in Session 9.

The additional three elements are:

People – ensuring the right people are in place, with appropriate attitudes as well as skills, to enable them to deal professionally with customers. People form part of the service offered, and deliver the means of customer satisfaction or dissatisfaction.

Process – ensuring that systems and processes involved in the delivery of the service are robust and effective enough to ensure a professional approach is achieved. Examples of these are appointment and queuing systems. How quickly can the customer get an appointment to see the dentist or the Bank Manager? How long do people stand in a queue before further assistance is provided? Is this acceptable to customers?

Physical evidence – this is often referred to as the "ambience" of the environment in which the service is offered. It includes such things as the layout, e.g. an open plan layout in a bank, the décor, the noise, appearance, smell, and ease of access.

Let's consider the way that a sports team, such as a football or basketball team, might develop an extended marketing mix for its "service".

Product
The service is the game the spectators watch.

Price
Normally some form of price differentiation is used, in that different prices are charged to occasional attendees than to regular customers. Season tickets will help deal with the "perishability" aspect of the service, in that seats in the stadium cannot be stored or resold after the game has been played.

Promotion
There are several aspects of promotion that might be used.

Advertising – TV commercials, merchandising to build the brand.

PR – around new players that are signed, and the approach to the game.

Personal selling – of tickets.

Sales promotion – free admission for children accompanied by their parents at selected matches, to encourage family attendance.

Place

What facilities are available in the stadium? Are travel facilities provided when the team is playing away?

People

The quality of the service is directly related to the people that deliver it. In the case of a sports game, customer service needs to be maintained, part of which may be provided by volunteers. Management need to ensure that standards are met by employed staff as well as volunteers by treating them well. It is also important that the team are treated specially, as they provide the entertainment and excitement that is the service offered.

Process

The "process" used to book tickets, or obtain refunds etc. must be efficient to maintain customer satisfaction.

Physical evidence

The environment within the stadium must be appropriate. Many football stadiums use the team colours in the seating areas. Cleanliness and safety are the most important factors for this sort of service. Much of the "ambience" is provided by the fans themselves. Programmes can provide a valued memento of the game, particularly for high status games such as cup competitions.

Activity 4.3

Think about the last time you purchased a "service" rather than a product. This may have been a visit to the cinema or the theatre, a sports event, insurance or legal advice, or a visit to the bank.

Make notes on the marketing mix that is in place for this service, identifying all seven "Ps".

Case Study – Interflora worldwide flower deliveries

Interflora is a non-profit making Trade Association, owned by its members, who are independent floristry businesses located throughout the world. These members are able to vote on issues at regional meetings and an Annual General Meeting. The aims of the Interflora organisation are encompassed in their mission statement.

'Our mission is to ensure that Interflora will always be the consumer's first choice for flowers and appropriate gifts. This means: recognising and responding to our customers' changing needs; providing a seamless service to our customers; leading our industry in innovation and design; continual improvement in quality, service, processes and costs, and enabling our employees and associates to give their best.'

The Interflora organisation consists of 58,000 florists worldwide delivering flowers to 146 countries – each and every one maintaining the stringent standards Interflora demands. From China to Russia, the USA to Europe, Interflora is able to deliver 'an expression of your thoughts through the most beautiful flowers imaginable.'

Starting with a fresh and original idea, Interflora blossomed into the world's largest and most popular flower delivery network. Today, the organisation boasts that no one can compete with its combination of creativity, experience and guaranteed quality.

The wide product range includes bouquets, hand-tied flowers, planted arrangements, floral arrangements, cut flowers, and unusual tailor-made floral gifts. Customers purchase their products for a variety of special occasions such as tokens of love, sympathy tributes, birthdays, new births, anniversaries and many others.

A customer selects and pays for a flower order in one of the participating florists who is a member of Interflora. The order is then communicated electronically to the nearest convenient Interflora member to the intended recipient, who then makes it up and delivers it to the destination required by the customer (which may be any place in the world). Interflora only uses floristry businesses that meet stringent criteria, such as good shop image, qualified staff, good variety and quality of stocks.

Interflora's trademark depicting the Roman god Mercury is one of the most recognised trademarks and symbols of quality and service in the world, and it helps form a common bond between the worldwide network of florists. The Interflora service is known by different trading names in different parts of the world, such as Fleurop in parts of Europe, and FTID in America, Canada and Japan. The name Interflora is used in the UK, Ireland and some other countries.

Source: Adapted from the Interflora web site.

From the Marketing Fundamentals Examination Paper, June 2000.

Questions

1. Describe the "people" element of the marketing mix that needs to exist for Interflora.

2. Describe the "process" element of the marketing mix that needs to exist for Interflora.

3. Describe the "physical evidence" element of the marketing mix that needs to exist for Interflora.

SUMMARY OF KEY POINTS

In this Session we have explored what is involved in the targeting and positioning stage of the marketing plan, and the importance of developing an appropriate marketing mix. The following key points were covered:

- There are three options for market coverage – differentiated marketing, undifferentiated marketing and concentrated marketing.

- Once decisions have been made about the segments to be targeted, appropriate marketing mixes need to be created for each segment.

- The traditional marketing mix consists of four elements – product, price, place and promotion.

- The marketing mix has been extended to allow for the fact that services differ from products – the three additional "Ps" are people, process and physical evidence.

Improving and developing own learning

The following projects are designed to help you develop your knowledge and skills further, by carrying out some research yourself. Feedback is not provided for this type of learning because there are no "answers" to be found, but you may wish to discuss your findings with colleagues and fellow students.

Project A
Find out if your organisation uses an undifferentiated, differentiated or concentrated approach to market coverage.

Project B
Select one of your target segments. What is the position your organisation is seeking to adopt in the customers' minds? Outline the elements of the traditional marketing mix as they apply to the segment you select.

Project C
If your organisation targets more than one segment, compare the marketing mix for an alternative segment to the one you selected in Project B. How much does it differ from the mix you saw in Project B?

Feedback to activities

Activity 4.1
1. Business purchase in boxes of 50.
2. Personal customer – age group 12-25, purchase as a gift.
3. Personal customer – age group 35-65, purchase as gift for a special occasion.

Activity 4.2

	Home furnishings	**Office furnishings**
Product	Range will keep pace with trends in colour schemes, and will need an attractive appearance. Range may include dining room suites, 3 piece suites, storage units, small tables, etc.	Range will include only a small number of standard colours, and will need to be durable and serviceable. Range may include desks, chairs, filing cabinets, storage units, etc.
Price	Price for quality.	Price for quality – however, a discounting structure may be introduced for bulk purchases.
Place	Retail outlets.	On site – delivery service from warehouse.
Promotion	"Home" consumer magazines, suitable exhibitions, direct marketing, web site.	Trade magazines, catalogues, personal selling, direct marketing, web site.

Activity 4.3

Answers will differ depending on the example you choose. An example for hairdressing is shown below.

Element of marketing mix	Description of service
Product	Range of hairdressing services, books showing trends in styles available.
Price	Prices displayed and fairly expensive. Service positioned as quality.
Place	Central High Street location, easily accessible. Range of salons covering local area.
Promotion	Advertising in local press. Money-off coupons for other services issued to existing customers.
People	Well trained – diplomas displayed, all pleasant and smiling.
Process	Computerised appointment system – records of customer history also kept.
Physical evidence	Clean and bright premises, comfortable seating while waiting, staff wearing same trousers and shirts.

Session 5

Product

Introduction

This Session is the first of five Sessions that tackle the elements of the marketing mix in some detail. This Session looks at all aspects of the product mix and the decisions a marketing manager needs to make in each respect. It explores the wider "bundle of benefits" that make up the product, and looks at the product life cycle concept and how this impacts on the other elements of the marketing mix.

> **LEARNING OUTCOMES**
>
> At the end of this Session you will be able to:
>
> - Demonstrate an awareness of products as "bundles of benefits" that deliver customer value and have different characteristics, features and levels.
>
> - Explain and illustrate the product life cycle concept and recognise its effects on marketing mix decisions.
>
> - Explain and illustrate the principles of product policy – branding, product lines, packaging and service support.
>
> - Explain the importance of introducing new products, and describe the processes involved in their development and launch.

The product

Products can be classified into several categories for both consumer and business-to-business markets.

The main categories for consumer goods are:

Convenience goods – sometimes also referred to as commodities; including milk, sugar, rice, potatoes and such items that may be included in a regular shopping list.

Shopping goods – these are more durable goods such as electrical appliances, furniture, cars, etc. In terms of buying decisions, the consumer will spend longer in the information search phase than they would for convenience goods.

Speciality goods – these are more exclusive items such as luxury cruises, designer clothes and jewellery. Buyer decisions about these products will follow an extensive search process, and prices for these items will be extremely high.

Business-to-business goods can also be classified, but the categories are very different.

Raw materials – such as rubber, metals etc. that are essential in the production of the final product.

Components – items that are used in the production of the final product, but have already been through some process, usually by a supplier.

Supplies – such as cleaning materials, stationery etc. which, whilst not involved in the production of the final product, are essential to the day-to-day running of the business.

Accessories – again, not part of the final product, but essential for the running of the business. These include office equipment, furniture etc.

Installations – these include the capital goods the company needs to make their final product, such as plant and machinery.

Product classifications need to be considered when putting together the marketing mix for the product, because they can tell the marketing manager something about how acceptable prices will be for each category, and how best to promote them.

The product, whatever category it falls into, is made up of a "bundle of benefits" that is offered as a package to the customer, and together they contribute significantly to the degree of value the customer places on the product.

This product "bundle" is made up of three levels.

The **core** product – this is the core benefit that the product or service offers. For example, the core benefit of a car is that it transports the user from A to B.

The **actual** product – these include the features and capabilities of the product, and also the brand name, packaging, quality and design. In a car these features deliver benefits such as comfort and safety.

The **augmented** product – this adds further value through warranties and guarantees, customer service or technical support, and delivery and installation if appropriate. The purchase of a new car, for example, often includes membership of a recovery service.

Each customer will place a different emphasis on the benefits offered. Some of the benefits may be irrelevant to them as individuals – the recovery service mentioned above is a good example of this. One purchaser may be pleased by this benefit, others may already be covered through their business or their partner, so it would not mean as much.

It is also worth noting that over time **actual** features become **core** features, and **augmented** features become **actual** features as customers' expectations grow. This means that companies have to introduce new features, usually in the **augmented** product, to distinguish it from competing products.

> **Activity 5.1**
>
> Look at advertisements for home computers. Identify the three levels of product benefits that are presented. Identify how these benefits may be perceived by:
>
> 1. Someone buying a PC for the first time.
> 2. Someone buying a replacement PC.

The Product Life Cycle (PLC)

A product, after being introduced to the marketplace, goes through a life cycle – from introduction, to growth, maturity and eventually decline. Each stage has different characteristics and therefore needs a different marketing mix. Marketing managers use their understanding of their products' life cycles to help manage their products (amendments to them, adjustments to pricing and promotional strategies) over time and to best effect.

The Product Life Cycle

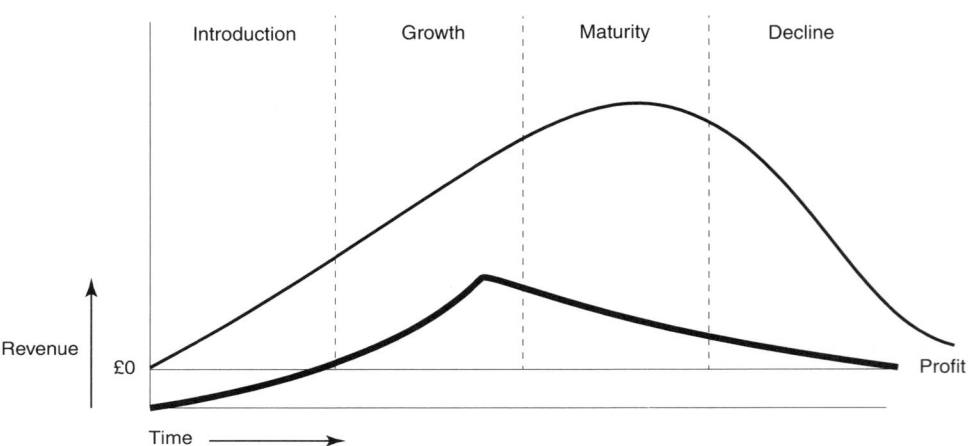

The Product Life Cycle (PLC) is based on the concept that a product has a life – birth (introduction), peak performance (growth/maturity) and death (decline). Many products now have a very short life cycle. They are likely to become obsolete quicker, due to new technologies or competitor activity.

The different stages of the life cycle are:

Pre-launch – no sales, but the product is attracting costs relating to development, marketing research etc.

Introduction – once launched, product sales produce a return on investment, but it is unlikely that there are profits. At this stage there will be few competitors. There is still a high failure rate at this stage of the PLC.

Growth – once people become aware of the product, sales grow rapidly and the product becomes profitable. More competitors will enter the market, particularly if access is "easy". Occasionally, companies that have developed products to this stage are targets for acquisition because of their success with the development of particular products. It is often seen as less costly for companies to "buy up" small companies that have developed successful products, than for them to take the risk of developing their own.

Maturity is reached in the market when growth slows but there is still potential for high sales and profits, as weaker competitors start to decline and the product is established with a significant market share. Marketing activity is based around strengthening the brand and reinforcing loyalty. Saturation is reached when only the strong competitors are left and the potential for sales growth is low.

Decline – this follows saturation. In the case of medicines and drugs, the product may be overtaken by one that is less expensive, more reliable, has fewer side effects, etc. There will be few customers left at this stage and companies need to make decisions, based on cost effectiveness, on when to remove a product from the market.

As can be appreciated, marketers need to adjust their strategies for communicating with consumers, clients, businesses and customers, and for pricing their products and getting them to market at different stages of the life cycle.

At the introductory stage products are moving from zero sales and the costs of developing the new product need to be recovered. Promotion needs to be heavy at the early stages to generate awareness of the product's features and benefits. Even if a high price is charged, sales need to be developed over time, and it is a while before any profits are generated. It also takes time to develop distribution outlets, and so products are not available at an optimum number of locations to achieve the required level of sales.

When a new product moves from the introductory stage of its life cycle to the growth stage, the good news is that sales are increasing. Unfortunately it also means that competitors are likely to be entering the market, and the company needs to be prepared to fight off the competition and establish the product's position in the marketplace.

At the growth stage the marketing mix may be adjusted as follows:

Product	A clearer picture of the segments to be targeted is emerging, and the company may need to introduce variations of the product to be able to penetrate the market more effectively.

Price   Depending on the extent of the competition, prices may be adjusted as initial development costs will have been recovered. If there is little competition, then prices are likely to remain static. If competition has moved in, the company may pass on some of its cost savings to the customer.

Promotion   Promotion will remain high, but the amount of advertising may be reduced slightly from the launch stage. Sales promotion might be used to improve the level of market share. The main message to be communicated will aim to emphasise the "position" of the product and the brand benefits.

Place   Distribution tends to intensify as products move into the growth phase, as the product is "accepted" in the marketplace and new outlets become easier to access. Companies need to ensure that they are able to supply the product at a rate to keep up with demand.

As it progresses on to the maturity stage further adjustments may be made.

Product   Further variations of the product may be made to try and stop it going into decline.

Price   Price reductions are made to retain market share and also to try and win market share from competitors.

Promotion   Activity will be focused towards reinforcing the message to encourage re-buys. Some emphasis may also be transferred to communicating with the trade to try and retain them as distributors.

Place   Attention is given to retaining the successful dealerships. Companies recognise that, if lost at this stage, they are unlikely to be able to win them back.

When the decline stage is reached, decisions have to be made about when to withdraw or replace the product, and what the likely effect will be. The number of distributors will normally be drastically reduced at this stage, promotion may cease, and prices may be reduced to shift remaining stock.

The product life cycle has been criticised for taking too simplistic a view of how products evolve. However, if it is looked upon as a framework to assist in the development of an effective marketing mix, then it can be useful.

Activity 5.2

A new Marketing Assistant has been appointed in your Department. She has come from the Sales Department, and your Manager has asked you to write some notes for her on the marketing mix, and how the product life cycle can be used to guide its development.

Produce a one-page briefing sheet for this new member of staff, giving some simple guidelines.

The product mix

The product mix is the whole group of products offered by an organisation to customers. The depth of the product mix refers to the number of products an organisation offers in each product line. The breadth of the product mix refers to the number of product lines offered. For example, a company such as Unilever offers washing powders, toothpaste, soap, deodorants and shampoos within its product mix. Each of these represent different product lines. Within one line they will offer a number of products under differing brand names, often targeting different segments.

In Session 9 of this Companion we will explore in-depth the marketing of services, in particular how they differ from tangible products. However, it is worth noting that even the most tangible products include characteristics or qualities that are service related, and so the extended marketing mix might be applied to any organisation. For example, if you buy a home PC it will include some form of guarantee, and you may also be offered some form of service contract, as well as technical support through a helpline.

Product policy

One benefit for a company offering a large product base is that it spreads the company's risk in terms of the money it has invested in developing the products in its product portfolio.

Each product goes through a product life cycle, and, in the case of toys for example, this life cycle is very short (on average one year). As one toy reaches the "decline" stage of the product life cycle, then the company needs to make a decision about whether gradually to phase out the product or withdraw it from the shelves.

One tool that can be useful in looking at the product portfolio as a whole, and the balance of products within it, is the Boston Consulting Group (BCG) Matrix. It is covered in more detail in the core text for this module. This model looks at the relative market share held by a product, against the rate of market growth. It categorises products in the following ways:

Stars – these are products with rapid growth potential, and which hold a dominant position in the market. They are still at a stage when the costs of promotion and fighting off the competition are high, but it is hoped that they will eventually move to a market leading position and bring in profits.

Cash cows – these products have been stars and still hold a dominant position in the market, but have moved into the maturity stage of their life cycle. They are generating cash that can help finance the development of "stars".

Dogs – these products have a low market share and poor growth potential. They may be making some profit. However, the decision the marketing manager needs to make is whether resources would be better directed to developing other, more profitable products.

Problem children (sometimes referred to as Question Marks) – this product is in a growing market, but holds a low market share. The marketer has to decide whether it is worth investing in the product to turn it into a "star", or whether to let it become a "dog". Turning these products into stars can be an expensive process.

The important factors in making such decisions are the amount of cash available and the amount of profit to be made.

Another issue with product growth is the danger that production will be unable to keep up with demand. Customers who are very disappointed through non-availability will tell others, and negative publicity and word-of-mouth communication can be very damaging to a firm's reputation in the future.

Product policy is concerned with such decisions as which products should be invested in, which should be dropped completely, how much emphasis should be placed on promoting each product within a range, which need to be developed, and how much emphasis should be placed on new product development.

New product development

The product life cycle, the need to stay ahead of the competition, and the analysis of the portfolio as a whole, all emphasise the need to develop new products to keep pace with customers' changing needs. It is a costly process. Many new products fail, and the life cycle model demonstrates how long it can take to develop a new product to the point where it makes a profit. It is an important area of marketing activity and much attention is paid to it.

The stages of the New Product Development process are as follows:

Idea generation – looking for product ideas and adaptations that help the organisation meet its objectives.

Screening ideas – considering ideas against business objectives and capabilities, and then matching them against customer needs. This stage may involve some marketing research.

Concept testing – at this stage the new product idea (usually with a written description and drawings if appropriate) is put before potential customers.

Business analysis – assessment of how the new product will fit with the existing product mix, and what contribution it will make to sales figures and profit (taking into account costs).

Product development – a lengthy and expensive phase that involves the development of prototypes. Depending on the success of this phase, work will then begin on branding, pricing and promotion.

Test marketing – the product is introduced on a small scale to a particular region (which ideally is representative of the final target market). There are many advantages to test marketing. It can help avoid the risk of product failure and valuable lessons can be learnt. However, there is a risk that competitors may try to copy the idea.

Commercialisation – this is where the lessons of the other stages are considered and a final plan put together to launch the product. A full marketing mix is developed to support the activity.

Marketing Fundamentals

Many things drive the development of new products. Using the airline industry as an example, Airbus have recently developed a new plane, the A380, and the factors that have influenced its development include:

- The forecast growth of global air traffic.
- Lack of available take-off and landing slots on some routes – congestion at major airports.
- Need for a reduction in operating costs for the airlines.
- The environment lobby – the need for greater fuel efficiency per passenger mile.
- Market pressure for lower fares.
- Consolidation in the industry and airline alliances.

Their new plane will carry much more cargo, or a higher number of passengers, and therefore will help them respond to these changing needs.

Factors affecting new product development

Information that might be useful before making any decision to develop new products includes secondary and primary data.

- Current market size, and what share do you already hold.
- Potential market size.
- Trends in market size and factors impacting upon it.
- Competitor details, and their activity in respect of new services.
- Potential competitors – are new competitors likely to enter the market?
- Customer needs – how are these changing, and what new services are likely to be needed.
- Pricing information – what do you need to charge to recoup any investment needed in developing new services, including that spent on research?
- Promotional information – what publications do our customers read? How else would it be appropriate to promote our services?

The above information would help you decide which new services are likely to be popular with customers, and how you can differentiate your service from that of your competitors. It would also help you establish whether or not the market was growing sufficiently to warrant expenditure on new services.

When you've made your decisions, you can then use the information to decide where and when to promote your services, and how much to charge.

The introduction of new products and services is a costly business, and many do not make it to market. The more accurate and in-depth related research is, the more likely they are to be successful.

Activity 5.3

Microsoft has recently developed the X-Box. Explain what factors may have led to its development. Look at www.xboxmagonline.co.uk to find out more about the product.

Activity 5.4

Your company manufactures and markets the goods shown in the following table, direct to consumers through its Internet site. Calculate the contribution to profit achieved by each product group for this current year.

Product group	Number sold	Price to consumer per unit	Fixed costs for year	Variable cost per unit
Fridge-freezer	7,500	€115	€357,000	€35
Washing machine	12,350	€330	€1,134,000	€175
Tumble dryer	6,250	€170	€378,000	€65
Dishwasher	3,500	€260	€189,000	€170
Microwave	650	€190	€42,000	€105

Branding

A brand forms part of the product's features and helps the customer identify its unique characteristics. A brand can be defined as a name, term, design, symbol or other feature that fulfils this purpose. Branding is becoming increasingly important as markets become more competitive, and can help differentiate one company's products from those of another. Customers perceive each brand to represent a certain level of quality. It can therefore be used by companies to help introduce new products to the market.

It is very important that organisations protect their brands, not only through trademarks, but also through continuing to present a useful and consistent message to customers and potential customers.

Packaging

How to package a product is an important decision for the marketer, and links closely to an understanding of buyer behaviour. It is said to fulfil four roles – protection, promotion, provision of information and convenience.

Protection – the marketer needs to think about the nature of the product and how best to protect it through its channel to market. For example, food items need to be protected from germs, and increasingly, be tamper proof. A music CD needs to be protected from becoming scratched or damaged, so that it will play and provide the benefit the customer is seeking.

Promotion – it is very important that the packaging is consistent with the brand and the image portrayed in all other forms of communication. This is covered further in Session 8 of this Companion.

Provision of information – packaging legislation dictates what **must** be on a package or its label. For example, packaging for cigarettes in the UK has to carry a government health warning. Provision of information can also become part of the product, in terms of telling customers and potential buyers how it may be used etc.

Convenience – the main characteristic here links to pricing. For example, reusable packs may enable cheaper prices to be offered for refills; smaller packs may make products more affordable; and multipacks may be offered with cost savings. The size of the package can also relate to buyer behaviour. For example, a large family may buy a large pack of detergent, whereas someone about to go on holiday may buy a very small pack for convenience when packing.

Looking at the above issues around packaging re-emphasises the links between the different elements of the marketing mix.

- Smaller packs and lower **prices**.

- Packaging and **promotion** of the brand.
- Multipacks for sub-division by wholesalers (**place**).

Case Study – Pleasure without the pain

Despite a declining yoghurt market, Müller Light's campaign has taken it to top position with a 12.8% share of the marketplace.

Müller Light's debut into the chilled desserts market took place in 1989. In 1999, it was relaunched with a new flavour and new advertising. Since then the brand has grown by 42% year on year, with profit growth in-line with increased volume. The Moving Average Target for 2000 was 12% of total yoghurt sales – a target reached by March that year.

The chilled desserts market is divided into four sectors – luxury, family, desserts and healthy. When Müller Light first launched into the "healthy" category in 1989, many marketing experts doubted it would be successful. At that time, the value-for-money offerings, multipacks, were responsible for the majority of the market. The introduction of a larger, 200g pot, was not expected to prove popular with dieters in particular, whose thinking revolved around portion control.

'Initially there was a little resistance to the idea of a larger portion because that wasn't what dieters were used to,' says Category Manager for healthy products, Ruth Konidaris. 'However, the market for Müller Light wasn't limited to this sector of the population. We were also successful in getting across the message that eating Müller Light was about eating more healthily. Consumers soon accepted that the product was a substantial eat, had virtually no fat and was low in calories. Dieters, in turn, were sold on the idea that a big pot was still good for them. After all, for someone thinking about food all the time, which dieters very often are, the idea of being able to eat a lot of something without piling on the calories was very, very appealing.'

A major relaunch

Despite the success already achieved, 1999 was identified as a key year in Müller Light's development, and a major relaunch was planned to take the brand into a market leadership position. The brand was given new packaging, a new flavour and new TV advertising. The new packaging was deemed to be important because although the product was made in the UK it had a very European style, which was off-putting for UK consumers. The launch of a new flavour, toffee, was also highly significant in achieving a greatly increased market share, quickly becoming Müller Light's second best-selling flavour, behind strawberry.

Advertising and promotion

To complete the new marketing package, Müller Light ran two new advertisements on television in both June and September 1999, spending £3.4 million. The ads, devised by Saatchi & Saatchi, focused on the pleasure-pain theory; i.e. you can't experience that much pleasure without someone suffering in some way as a result.

The first was set in a park and centred on a woman eating Müller Light on a bench, while another asks 'Should you be eating that?' As the first woman continues to enjoy her yoghurt, a man nearby falls off his bicycle, gets bitten by a dog, stung by a swarm of bees and struck by lightning! The end line was 'So much pleasure, where's the pain?'

The second ad ran on similar lines and both were repeated throughout the year. Research to measure the effectiveness of the advertising campaign showed that the percentage of 16-44 year old housewives (the target audience) acknowledging Müller Light as their favourite yoghurt rose from 21% pre-advertising to 30% by July 2000. By August 2000, 57% of people asked to recall the end line could do so.

The millennium was an added bonus for the brand. 'At the start of a new millennium, consumers were taking their New Year resolutions, such as losing weight, more seriously than usual,' says Konidaris. 'We anticipated the impact of this and made more extensive use of the slimming press at this time, including offering money-off coupons to encourage people to give the brand a try. Circulation figures of slimming magazines rose sharply during this period, so the strategy proved to be highly effective.'

Müller Light grew to achieve a market share of 12.8% against the other leading brand's 8%. These results were achieved against the background of a declining yoghurt market in 1999. 'We have established a strong relationship with consumers,' says Konidaris. 'What was initially perceived to be our weakness, the larger pot size, is now viewed as part of our generosity and has become one of our strengths.'

Source: 'Pleasure without the pain', *Marketing Business*, May 2001.

> **Questions**
>
> 1. What developments were made to the product in 1999, 10 years after its launch?
>
> 2. What was the major risk Müller were taking in terms of the launch in 1989?
>
> 3. What did the newly developed product achieve through its relaunch?

> ## SUMMARY OF KEY POINTS
>
> In this Session we have explored all aspects of the product mix and covered the following key points:
>
> - Products consist of a full bundle of benefits that can be offered to the customer.
>
> - Products are said to go through a "life cycle", the stages of which often require adjustments to be made to the elements of the marketing mix.
>
> - When products reach the maturity stage of the product life cycle, decisions need to be made as to whether the product's life should be extended, or whether it should be discontinued.
>
> - To keep up with changing customer needs, new products must be developed, and there is a defined process for this development process.

Improving and developing own learning

The following projects are designed to help you develop your knowledge and skills further, by carrying out some research yourself. Feedback is not provided for this type of learning because there are no "answers" to be found, but you may wish to discuss your findings with colleagues and fellow students.

Project A

Choose one of your company's products, and break it down into its component parts – its core, actual and augmented benefits.

Project B

Try to identify where the product sits on its life cycle curve. If it has reached maturity, identify any efforts that have been made to prolong its life cycle through adaptation of the product itself, or through promotion.

Project C

Look at the range of products offered by your company, or one you know well. Using the categories of the Boston Consulting Group (BCG) Matrix, identify the Stars, Cash Cows, Problem Children and Dogs.

Feedback to activities

Activity 5.1

Answers to this are not as simple as they may seem. The categories of first time buyer and repurchaser give us some clues, but we do not know how experienced either purchaser is. Assuming the repurchaser knows more about the product, the product might be broken down as follows:

Product benefits	New buyer	Re-buyer
Core	PC for home computing and connection to the Internet.	PC for home computing and connection to the Internet.

Product benefits	New buyer	Re-buyer
Actual	Dell. Smartstep 100D. Simple system. Value price. 1ghz. Compact mini tower. 20Gb hard drive. Internet. Email. Word processing.	Dell. Dimension 4400. Superior performance. Reasonable price. 2ghz. Expandable mini tower. 120Gb hard drive. Advanced video graphics. Multiple product functionality. Video editing.
Augmented	Choice of software bundle. Technical support. Service warranty. Standard limited warranty. Credit facilities available.	Free delivery. Free tax software package. Choice of software bundle. Technical support. Service warranty. Standard limited warranty. Credit facilities available.

The new buyer may perceive the technical support and service package as more important. The repurchaser, who will already have some software and some knowledge of setting up and using a PC, may perceive the fact that they have a choice over whether or not to buy software to be more important than the technical support.

Activity 5.2

Important points to bear in mind are the fact that your "audience" for this document is new, and that the briefing paper should include "simple" guidelines.

Product life cycle

Stages – introduction, growth, maturity, decline.

Characteristics of stages and implications for the marketing mix

	Introduction	Growth	Maturity	Decline
Product	New.	Some modifications made.	Improvements made to maintain life cycle.	Decisions about when to withdraw product.
Price	Profits negative because of development costs.	Prices maintained and profits start to improve, then competitors enter market and force prices down.	Profits continue to decline and heavy competition in marketplace.	Prices may be cut to shift stock.
Place	Limited outlets.	More outlets developed.	More outlets developed.	Only a few distributors retained.
Promotion	Heavy and expensive to raise awareness and grab market share before competitors enter market.	Heavy use of advertising continues, sales promotion often used to encourage purchase.	Promotion to trade used as well as to consumers.	Promotion usually cut.

Activity 5.3

Factors leading to product development include:

Competition – games machines are strong competitors to PCs in terms of games.

Customers – the portability of games machines is popular with target market.

Market potential – the development of the product will give the opportunity to develop and market more sophisticated computer games.

Product benefit – extends the market, as not all of the target market would have the need for a PC.

Activity 5.4

Product group	Contribution to profit
Fridge-freezer	€243,000
Washing machine	€780,250
Tumble dryer	€278,250
Dishwasher	€126,000
Microwave	€13,250

Session 6

Price

Introduction

Price is an important element of the marketing mix. When set, it will help position the product or service, and reflect many factors from both inside and outside the organisation. This Session covers both these factors and their influence on the decision process, and also the pricing policies and tactics that are available to the organisation.

> **LEARNING OUTCOMES**
>
> At the end of this Session you will be able to:
>
> - Explore the range of internal and external factors that influence pricing decisions.
> - Identify and illustrate a range of pricing policies and tactics that are adopted by organisations as effective means of competition.

Factors affecting pricing decisions

An organisation has to take many factors into account when deciding on its pricing policy. These include the size of the organisation and its objectives, the level of demand for the product, the amount of competition in the marketplace, as well as how much it costs to produce and distribute the product.

Company and marketing objectives

Everything that the marketing department does should reflect corporate objectives, and, in turn, marketing objectives. An organisation that is looking to grow market share may need to reduce prices in the short term, whereas an organisation that is looking to improve profitability would not achieve its objective by following the same pricing strategy.

Company resources

Decisions about prices have to take account of the level of resources available to the organisation over a period of time. For example, price competition is a familiar sight in retailing, and supermarkets have fiercely engaged in it from the late 1990s onwards. In order to do so they have to drive down the costs of supplies and the costs within their own operations, so that they can be more flexible in their pricing decisions.

The main danger of price wars is that organisations cannot sustain the downward spiral of prices, as competitors find new ways of producing more efficiently and cheaply. This risk is particularly acute in undifferentiated markets, for example petrol, where the only difference between competing products is price. If one major player in the market is forced to raise prices, rivals may continue to hold down theirs to gain additional volume.

Product costs

Price and cost are different. **Price** is how much a company sells its product for; **cost** is how much it costs to make and get to market. Although costs are not the only factor for the marketer in setting prices, they are a significant factor in the pricing decision, and the cost structure of the firm must be considered when setting prices.

With respect to pricing generally, there are three main measures of cost structure that are relevant: the ratio of fixed to variable costs; the relationship between costs and volume; and the costs an organisation has compared to those of its competitors. Techniques such as break-even analysis are extremely useful in making price decisions.

The break-even point for a product is the point at which its production costs equal the revenue made by selling the product. The figure is arrived at by making the following calculation:

$$\text{Break-even point} = \frac{\text{Fixed costs}}{\text{Price} - \text{variable costs}}$$

In a company, product X is sold for £200 per unit. It has variable costs of production of £120 per unit. Therefore the contribution made to fixed costs by each unit sold is £80. If total fixed costs, including marketing and recouping Research and Development (R&D) = £240,000, then the break-even point is calculated as:

$$\frac{£240,000}{£80} = 3,000 \text{ units}$$

This means that the company needs to sell a minimum of 3,000 units just to cover its fixed costs. At this stage it is not making a profit. For every unit sold above the break-even point, each unit still contributes £80, but as the fixed costs have now been covered it is all profit.

Cutting costs in an effort to be able to reduce prices can lead to a reduction in the quality of services offered, or a lack of innovation, as operations become internally focused on reducing overheads and costs. Therefore, those who survive a price war may be leaner, but they are not necessarily fitter, and may well have lost sight of customer needs. Customer loyalty is difficult to sustain during price wars, as buyers are encouraged to evaluate alternatives on price alone.

Market demand

This is extremely important to the marketer. There is a point where the market will no longer accept the level of price set for a product or service. The marketer needs to think about how they will cope with supply if the price is too low, and what will happen to the volume of sales if the price is too high.

We can talk about price elasticity of demand. When the demand for a product does not change much when a price change is made, it is referred to as being price inelastic. When changes in price result in relatively large changes in the level of demand, this is referred to as being price elastic.

When looking at demand, it is important to revisit the buyer's perception of the value being offered by the product or service (see Session 1). The whole marketing mix, as well as the target market for a product, will affect this perception.

Competition/market structure

Different levels of competition will affect organisations that work in different markets. In markets where there are few competitors, the largest companies tend to take a lead that the other companies have to follow. Where there are many companies offering very similar products, then competition on price will be much more acute.

When faced with a high level of competition, companies often try to differentiate their product through quality, advertising or special product features, so that they are not pushed out of business by the "price setting" firms.

Companies also have to think about how easy it is for new competitors to enter the market, as this may also impact on their pricing decisions.

Legal factors

Companies need to consider whether their pricing decisions are legal. In the UK, the Competition Act, 2000, stops companies using practices that restrict competition. These practices would include agreements to fix prices and impose minimum resale prices. It also forbids the use of cartels, which is when firms within a particular industry agree to set prices at a specific level.

Distribution

The channels that a company uses to get its products to market also have an impact on its pricing decisions. For example, a company that uses agents or distributors needs to allow for the fact that they too will look to put a margin on the price, whereas a company that markets direct will save on this cost and can either pass it on to the consumer, or improve their own margin on the product.

Other factors

Pricing decisions also have to consider what stage in the product life cycle the product has reached. New product pricing strategy is covered in the next section. Adjustments may be needed to maintain the product at the maturity stage. When it goes into decline, reductions may be made to maintain sales, and finally, prices may be cut severely to shift stock.

Activity 6.1

Tom's Bakery makes iced birthday cakes, which they sell for £7.50 each. The fixed costs involved in making these cakes are £1,500, and the variable costs are £1.50 per cake.

Calculate the break-even point for the birthday cakes.

Pricing policies

Pricing policy is the term used to describe the overall approach that an organisation takes to pricing. It covers such decisions as how they price against competitors (just above or just below their main competitor); and whether or not they will use price promotions.

When looking to set a price, the marketer goes through several stages.

- Consideration of company objectives.
- Consideration of desired positioning of product and target segment.
- Consideration of what price the target market will carry.
- Consideration of market demand, as well as cost and profit relationships.
- Consideration of the competitive situation, and what competitors charge.
- Consideration of product life cycle stage.
- Consideration of overall marketing mix.
- Decision on price.

In particular, when looking to launch a new product into the market, there are two main pricing strategies. **Market penetration**, which involves setting a low price to gain a high volume of sales, or **market skimming**, which involves setting the price at a higher level and positioning the product to "skim" the top of the market.

> **Activity 6.2**
> Explain the eight stages a marketing manager will go through in setting a price for a product or service.

Pricing tactics or methods

There are various pricing methods that can be selected by a marketer to help the organisation compete. For example, it is extremely rare for an organisation to offer only one product, and marketers are therefore able to adjust prices across the product portfolio to maximise profits. There are several approaches to this.

Product line pricing

Products across a product line have their prices "stepped" according to the difference in their cost to produce, their benefits or features, and the way their competitors price their equivalents. For example, various toothpastes are priced differently even though they are offered by the same company.

Optional product pricing

This is a tactic that involves the sale of a basic product with a range of optional extras. Cars, for example, are offered as a basic model, or with the options of air-conditioning, tinted windows, alloy wheels, etc.

Product bundle pricing

Products are bundled together and sold cheaper than when sold separately. Multipacks of crisps are one example of this, where families can gain small cost savings when buying packs containing six or twelve individual packs.

Methods for setting a price, whether of a product or product portfolio, include:

Cost-plus pricing

This a simple pricing method that involves calculating the costs involved in producing a product (including the research and development costs), then adding a fixed percentage profit to these costs to arrive at a price. This method does not suit the marketer, as it has no consideration of what the market considers value for money. It is used widely in contracting, particularly where buyers are strong and effectively set the price they are willing to pay.

Demand-based pricing

This is the most marketing orientated way of setting a price. Consideration is given to what potential customers are prepared to pay for a product through carrying out primary research.

Competitor parity

This is where prices are matched to the competition. This means that products must be differentiated from the competition in some way, so that something other than price gives you a competitive advantage.

Psychological pricing

This is the name given to the method of pricing that involves setting prices at set price points, such as $399.95, or £19.99, in the hope that customers may feel they are paying less than if the price was $400 or £20.

> **Activity 6.3**
>
> Why should the marketer be aware of competitors' prices? How might they use this knowledge when arriving at a price for their own product?
>
> Produce a bar chart, using spreadsheet software or the chart facility in Word, showing the price of one of your products in comparison to its two main competitors.

Case Study – Battle of the brands

The 1998 football World Cup, held in France, was a global stage for the biggest and the best. As might be expected all the top football teams were at France '98. However, another competition was taking place behind the relatively insignificant struggle between the likes of England and Argentina – between the two sportswear brands Nike and Adidas.

Even the most fleeting trip to Paris firmly brought home the point that football is increasingly the plaything of the huge sportswear corporations. At stake is the small matter of being the biggest sportswear company in the world. The ground on which this battle will increasingly be fought is football. In the last three years the market for endorsements and advertising deals has exploded. The reasons for this are many and varied (after all, football has never been this big, and just keeps on getting bigger), but they all boil down to one key factor. The emergence of Nike as a major player.

'We are very new to football, but we see that as an advantage. We can bring product innovation to the sport, be inventive, take a whole new perspective to football. Already the game is very important to Nike'. So says Debbie Cox, PR Manager of Nike UK. Nike is rumoured to have spent £35 million on the '98 World Cup alone. It booked up strategic poster sites around France more than two years before the event.

The deployment of this bottomless war chest has quickly brought Nike access to the most exclusive centres of the football world. 'We have been able to cultivate our relationship with some of the key players,' enthuses Cox. 'For example Ronaldo (one of Brazil's top players) was actively involved in the design and testing of our latest boot, the Mercurial'.

'Nike is very much the new kid on the block', says Martin Cannon of the Institute of Sports Sponsorship and head of Cannon Communications. 'It is brash, pushy, a bit of a rebel, while Adidas is very official, a stable, established sports brand for people who are very serious about their football. Nike can call on huge resources to fund their marketing campaigns, and they can also justify the amount of money spent, because in advertising terms the "reach" is so high. The vast majority of people watching a football match are going to be interested in buying sportswear'.

This is the key. When compared to the sums spent on developing and promoting football boots, the market for them in Britain is pretty small. Each year just over a million pairs are sold, at a combined cost of approximately £60 million.

Now, after the latest boom, the marketplace looks rather crowded. Even Adidas, who remain leaders of the British sportswear sector after several strong years, admit there is likely to be a shakedown. However, unless the world of fashion says differently, no one in their right mind is going to go "down the pub" in a pair of football boots! But when Nike pay Ian Wright (a top British football player) to play in their boots, or when Umbro sign up Alan Shearer (the England captain in the '98 World Cup) for £25,000 a year, they are primarily concerned with promoting the brand not the boot. This is where the real money lies. Put the right logo on a pair of trainers, T-shirt or bag and it will sell well.

Market research company Mintel estimate that the British sportswear market is worth £1.7 billion, which includes 20 million trainers sold every year. Nike have built up a $9 billion-a-year global business on the basis of trainers that can be sold for £80 a pair, but probably cost as little as £1.20 to actually make in a factory in Thailand.

A leading London marketing consultant states 'It's reached saturation point. A few years ago everyone bought Nike, no one bought Adidas. But the trendsetters have moved on. Those 16 to 20 year olds who lead the market won't be seen dead in the same trainers as their parents. To be honest the trainer is starting to look rather tired'.

This passage has been adapted from an article featured in BBC Match of the Day (MOTD) Magazine, August/September 1998, and has been reproduced with kind permission from BBC Worldwide Ltd.

Source: Case Study first used in Marketing Fundamentals Examination Paper, December 1999.

Questions

1. Identify the types of information that will be useful in setting the price for a new pair of football boots.

2. Suggest the most appropriate pricing method for the new football boots.

SUMMARY OF KEY POINTS

In this Session we have explored various aspects of the price mix, and covered the following key points:

- Internal factors affecting pricing decisions include company and marketing objectives, company resources, production costs and distribution costs.
- External factors affecting pricing decisions include market demand, legal factors and competitive/market structures.
- There is an eight-stage process that marketers should go through to arrive at their pricing policy.
- There are two main pricing strategies appropriate for the pricing of new products – penetration pricing and market skimming.
- There are various methods for setting prices available to an organisation, not all of which are marketing oriented.

Improving and developing own learning

The following projects are designed to help you develop your knowledge and skills further, by carrying out some research yourself. Feedback is not provided for this type of learning because there are no "answers" to be found, but you may wish to discuss your findings with colleagues and fellow students.

Project A

Find out what pricing methods are used by your organisation. Who is involved in making the decisions?

Project B
Draw up a table comparing the prices of your main products against those of your three main competitors.

Project C
Referring to the table you have prepared in Project B, make notes about internal and external factors that might explain your prices against those of your competitors.

Feedback to activities

Activity 6.1
The break-even point is 250 birthday cakes.

Activity 6.2
1. Consideration of company objectives – prices need to be set at a level where they can contribute to overall company objectives.

2. Consideration of desired positioning of product and target segment – the price needs to be at an appropriate level to suggest the position selected.

3. Consideration of what price the target market will carry – pricing too high will reduce the volume of sales.

4. Consideration of market demand, as well as cost and profit relationships – demand for the product will probably reduce proportionately to the price.

5. Consideration of the competitive situation, and what competitors charge – the company needs to consider how they will respond to competitors prices. They could undercut them, maintain a position of quality, or target an alternative segment.

6. Consideration of product life cycle stage – will the product's stage in the PLC allow prices to be maintained?

7. Consideration of overall marketing mix – how can the other elements of the mix help stop reductions in prices?

8. Decision on price – final decision made and communicated.

Activity 6.3

It is important to monitor competitor prices so that you know how to respond.

The information can be used to anticipate the competitor's strategy and try to counter it, to stay competitive, to undercut, to target a different segment if necessary, or to shape the promotional activity so that prices do not need to be cut.

Your bar chart will be specific to your own company and market.

Session 7

Place

Introduction

This Session explores the various channels of distribution, including the Internet, that are available to companies to enable them to get their products to market. It also considers the factors that affect the decisions marketing managers need to take about the way products reach customers.

> **LEARNING OUTCOMES**
>
> At the end of this Session you will be able to:
>
> - Define channels of distribution, intermediaries and logistics, and understand the contribution they make to the marketing effort.
> - State and explain the factors that influence channel decisions and the selection of alternative distribution channel options, including the effects of new information and communications technology.

Channels of distribution

There are several possible channels to market available to most companies when they select a distribution network. These include using agents, distributors, wholesalers, retailers, and going direct to the consumer. Recently, the Internet is being used as a direct route to market, but like all channels, this has its disadvantages as well as advantages. These channels are explored further below.

Agents – these can be manufacturers' agents, selling agents, brokers, or commission merchants. They do not usually take title or ownership of the products or services, but receive a commission for facilitating the exchange between a seller and a buyer.

Distributors – these on the other hand do usually take ownership of the goods on which they charge a mark-up, handling fee or the manufacturer's recommended price (which includes a margin). Not all distributors deal with end users. The channels listed below are sometimes referred to as distributors.

Wholesalers – these perform a wide range of functions for the manufacturer at one end of the chain, and for the retailer at the other end. These services/functions usually more than compensate for the proportion of profit they take from the manufacturer.

Functions for the manufacturer include:

- Promotional activity.
- Warehousing, storage and "breaking up" of stock.
- Some of the transport arrangements.
- Inventory control.
- Feedback of information, particularly about competitor activity and prices.
- Credit control.

For the retailer they include:

- Passing on of information.
- Provision of a "one-stop" shopping environment for the smaller retailer.
- Making smaller purchases available.
- Fast delivery/collection facilities.

Retailers – these include the corner shop, the High Street shop, supermarkets, and convenience stores. Retailers deal almost exclusively with end-consumers of goods, or customers purchasing consumer goods for their family and friends, rather than with businesses.

Direct routes – this involves the manufacturer or producer dealing direct with either the end-consumer or business buying their product. It can be achieved through direct mail order (often with a catalogue), the Internet, or through a company's own sales force. Fulfilment of orders is still key in this method of distribution, and this can be run in-house or outsourced.

Intermediaries – an intermediary is someone who promotes the products or services of one company to another company or to end-consumers. They are sometimes referred to as "middlemen". Retailers and wholesalers are intermediaries.

Logistics – this is the term used to describe the physical distribution of products through the channel. For example, decisions need to be made about warehousing and transportation of goods.

Channel conflict

When selecting a distribution network, care must be taken to make sure "channel conflict" does not arise. Companies looking to cut costs by using the Internet rather than a middleman, such as an agent or wholesaler, need to consider the additional benefits offered by their existing channel to market that might be lost if substituted by the Internet (this process of cutting out the middleman is referred to as disintermediation).

Let's consider whether the Internet can offer advantages over catalogue-based direct marketing.

Let's look at the advantages first.

- The cost of producing a catalogue and associated mailing costs are high.
- New customers may be attracted to a web site through banner ads, search engines or off-line publicity – this is not possible with a catalogue.
- Customers who use the Internet often want convenience and immediacy. In comparison, having to wait for a catalogue to arrive is slow and frustrating.

The disadvantages are:

- Not all households have access to the Internet. Retailers may know that some of their existing customers shop online, but these may still be only a small proportion of all their customers.
- The cost of setting up a web site can be high. John Lewis took the decision to acquire the UK division of Buy.com in order to get the technological infrastructure and expertise it needed. Future updates may be less costly, but systems need to be in place to ensure that the site is regularly updated and interesting, or customers may not return.
- There is still a high level of distrust among consumers about buying over the Internet, so valuable orders may be lost.

In both cases the fulfilment of orders needs to be efficient. An established retailer's customers will have expectations of high standards of service, and an Internet-based service must meet or exceed those expectations.

Companies also need to consider different cultural attitudes when looking to market internationally. This aspect is covered more fully in Session 12.

For example, in contrast to Europe, when considering using the Internet as a direct channel to market in Japan, offering the possibility of collecting the goods from bricks and mortar outlets will offer distinct benefits over the direct delivery route. This is mainly a result of different attitudes to the use of credit cards. In Europe, credit cards are routinely used to purchase goods. However, borrowing money is considered "shameful" in Japan, and so customers will be reluctant to use credit cards to purchase goods direct from the supplier over the Internet. If they are able to collect their goods from an intermediary (sometimes referred to as a bricks and mortar outlet – because of the physical nature of the store, as compared to the "virtual" store on the Internet), then they can pay by other means when collecting their purchases.

This route to market also offers other advantages.

- Where customers are out at work all day, it can be more convenient to collect the goods they have selected from a local store, which is open longer hours than they work.
- Customers who are worried about credit card fraud can pay by other means.
- Customers who are concerned about illegal access to their financial details over the Internet are also reassured by being able to pay be other means.

Activity 7.1

Draw a diagram representing the following channels to market:

1. Manufacturer selling direct to a business.
2. Manufacturer selling to businesses through an agent.
3. Producer selling to a wholesaler, who sells to a retailer, who sells to a customer.

Factors affecting channel decisions

The factors affecting the choice of distribution channel and method of transportation include:

Where the market is and the likely sales volume

Is our market spread over a large geographical area? Is it well contained in one region of a country? Also, what volume of sales are we likely to make to any one area? These issues will have a major impact on whether we outsource transportation, or use our own fleet of vehicles.

Product characteristics

Fragile and perishable products need shorter channels so as to minimise spoilage. When transporting overseas, perishable products may warrant the higher cost of air-freight, because balanced against the cost of spoilage on a longer sea journey it may actually work out cheaper.

Competitor activity

Can you achieve a competitive advantage by choosing an alternative route to market?

Cost

The organisation's resources will obviously impact on the choice of distribution channel, but the example used in "product characteristics" is also relevant.

Reliability

How much control do you need to have over the channel? If there is a need for tight control to protect the brand for example, then a shorter chain will be more manageable.

Security issues

High-value items will often demand exclusive distribution through specialist outlets, or via mail order.

Level of customer service involved

Does the customer demand a fast delivery service? A courier service may be needed. How complex is the buying decision? In the case of complex products or services, consumer markets tend to use retailers, so that there is face-to-face contact and products or services can be properly explained. In business-to-business markets we may use our own sales force to pass on expert knowledge.

Legal issues

Legislation such as the Competition Act, Fair Trading Act, Trade Descriptions Act, Data Protection Act and the Consumer Protection Act, all impact on channel decisions. For example, the Data Protection Act affects companies that hold personal customer data for direct distribution. In the past, some wholesalers and dealers have refused to implement anti-competitive practices that manufacturers have tried to impose on them, and as a result have been blacklisted by the manufacturers. This is now illegal under the Competition Act.

Activity 7.2

Consider the channel from farm to consumer via a local market or supermarket, and the channel from a photocopier manufacturer to a business. How do the above factors influence each channel?

Channel decisions in action

Direct marketing

Computer manufacturer Dell offers computers for sale through direct marketing to customers. The main advantages Dell's production and distribution systems offer over a competitor such as Compaq's are:

1. **Cost savings**

    They use "Just in Time" (JIT) production processes, building machines to order, and not ordering stock in until it is needed in the short term. This means they hold cash longer (earning interest), and only hold small amounts of stock (saving money on storage space, and lessening the risk of it becoming out-dated). Dell also does not have to cover a dealer "mark-up" on price, and therefore saves further costs that can be passed on to the customer.

2. **Efficient delivery direct to customers**

    Selling direct to customers means that, providing they use a good logistics company to make their deliveries, Dell can get a customised product to the customer earlier than its competitors can.

Both of the above measures need an effective relationship marketing strategy, which includes reliable and trusted suppliers, both of component parts and delivery services. If Dell is able to maintain its increase in market share with this strategy until the industry price war ends (in spite of cutting back its staff), then it will have used its relationships effectively, to the benefit of all involved.

Franchising

Franchise operations are a common distribution strategy in fast food chains such as Perfect Pizza and McDonald's. They are usually based on an arrangement whereby the franchiser licenses the use of a strong brand image to a franchisee, who then runs a business within the limitations of the franchise agreement. The agreement is necessary to protect the original brand image.

There are advantages to both franchisee and franchiser. One gets the benefit of a major company and a well-known brand, and the other gains the ability to expand their network of outlets rapidly.

Papa John's for example, were able to expand quickly into the UK market using the local knowledge of franchisees. It decided that franchising was a much cheaper option than opening its own outlets overseas, and it was also able to avoid the costly relocation of its own staff internationally.

Franchising also involves less financial risk, with a constant flow of new money into the business as new franchisees "buy-in". This capital can then be used for improved advertising and communication of the whole brand.

Franchisees are generally more committed than managers to running an outlet effectively, as they have invested their own funds. However, it is not as risky as starting a new business, as they have the support of the franchiser should any business problem emerge. With a strong brand such as Perfect Pizza or Papa John's they are also virtually guaranteed to attract customers in numbers right from the start.

Franchisees in this business are likely to see a return on their investment within three years, which is much sooner than usual within the industry. This is endorsed by the fact that there are many "multiple franchisees"; those operating more than one outlet. Franchisees are unlikely to invest more money if they have not had a good experience with their first outlet.

Out-of-town retailing

The past two decades have seen an enormous growth in supermarkets and out-of-town shopping parks, resulting in a steady decline in local shops. Large retailers can offer choice and low prices, due to their ability to employ economies of scale, making it very difficult for their smaller rivals to compete. This has led to small communities being left with no local facilities as their local shops close. Many people feel that this is a backward step socially, as the larger retailers may be efficient, but lack the personal touch of the local shopkeeper. Changes in consumer lifestyles are the major reason for this growth in multiple retailers. Consumers want to shop at a time that is convenient for them, and they want to purchase essential goods at one shop rather than having to visit a number of smaller outlets, such as the butcher, the baker, the candlestick maker, etc. They are mobile and able to choose where they want to shop, rather than being restricted to the immediate locality. The Internet has also increased the opportunities for consumers to enjoy home shopping, even for fast moving consumer items.

The major supermarket chain Tesco has invested in new stores in the West Midlands region of the UK. This is a very welcome initiative, creating new jobs at a challenging time for an area suffering from the decline of its traditional industries. High unemployment often leads to a decline in local communities, as consumer's disposable income decreases. Tesco have formed local partnerships to ensure that the local long-term unemployed are targeted for the new jobs, as part of its commitment to regeneration. Retail jobs often boost local economies by acting as a catalyst for further investment.

Many large retailers have also stimulated demand by making shopping a more family friendly experience. Most offer family friendly restaurants, trolleys that allow parents to strap small children in safely (so the parents can concentrate on the shopping), and have other distractions for the under 12s. For example, IKEA provide crèche facilities and entertainment, such as films and ball pools, where children can be left for a certain period of time. The cost of this and the staff to supervise it is offset by the increase in volume (numbers through the door) and the additional shopping time it gives adults.

Organisations are very aware that they need to be good neighbours in the community. Out-of-town retailers, such as Tesco and IKEA, try to ensure that their presence causes minimal disruption to traffic flows, their car parks and surrounding land are clean and pleasant to look at, and that they are not perceived as causing pollution.

Internet shopping

As previously mentioned, the Internet offers retailers further opportunities to sell. E-shopping is already a well-established concept and is set to grow as consumers gain confidence in the service element – delivery.

Often those companies first in the market gain a competitive advantage and are seen to be ahead of the rest. It is important for large retailers to be seen to use technology to improve services for customers, and this includes in-store services as well as e-services. Technology can be used to improve the speed and reliability of checkout services, stock control, and the provision of information about sales promotions. Customers of Sainsbury's supermarkets can use their loyalty cards to electronically access in-store services such as money-off coupons, recipes and information about what they can "spend" their loyalty bonuses on (such as cinema tickets or vouchers).

Many organisations also recruit online by placing job advertisements on their web sites. Some allow people to apply online, whilst others provide a point of contact to request application forms.

Activity 7.3

Visit www.tesco.com and www.sainsbury.co.uk . List the benefits they offer the customer through shopping online, and the efforts they are making to make the shopping experience as similar to visiting one of their stores as possible, but with added convenience.

Case Study – Supermarket car sales

The large supermarket chains in Europe are looking for permission to sell cars. Currently, the European Commission is warning that in the long term, allowing supermarkets and Internet dealers to sell cars will reduce consumer choice and increase prices.

The debate has recently escalated because, from 2003, it is intended to remove a regulation that currently requires all car dealerships to provide repair services. This is all that is preventing the supermarkets offering cars for sale. However, the European Commission has stated that the manufacturers should be allowed to exclude supermarkets and Internet dealers from the relaxation of the rule.

The purpose of this new rule is to strengthen competition across both dealer networks and across the EU, and so it should therefore benefit the consumer. However, this would seem to be in contradiction to their decision to restrict supermarkets and Internet dealers. Surely the supermarkets would mean increased availability and lower prices, as would Internet dealers? The Commission acknowledges that this may be the case, but only in the short term. They fear that eventually supermarkets would be able to use their enormous buying power to increase prices, and, if traditional car dealers were forced out of business, there would then be less consumer choice, and reduced customer satisfaction.

In addition, the car manufacturers could be forced to reduce the choice available to consumers, if there were only a limited number of dealers to whom they had to provide large volumes of cars.

Source: This Case Study was compiled from secondary sources.

Questions

1. What advantages and disadvantages might car manufacturers gain through using supermarkets as part of their channel to market?

2. What advantages and disadvantages might car manufacturers gain through using Internet dealers as part of their channel to market?

3. What advantages and disadvantages might car manufacturers gain through staying with the traditional channel of dealerships?

SUMMARY OF KEY POINTS

In this Session we have explored various options available to marketing managers to get their products to market, and covered the following key points:

- The method of distribution selected by the company affects the other elements of the marketing mix.

- The channel to market needs to be designed with the customer in mind.
- Using the Internet and cutting out intermediaries can add cost rather than reduce it.
- Retailing is no longer limited to city centres or High Street shopping areas.

Improving and developing own learning

The following projects are designed to help you develop your knowledge and skills further, by carrying out some research yourself. Feedback is not provided for this type of learning because there are no "answers" to be found, but you may wish to discuss your findings with colleagues and fellow students.

Project A
Draw a diagram of the channels used by your organisation in getting its products to market.

Project B
Find out how your organisation's distribution policy affects the price of its products.

Project C
Talk to your Marketing Manager about the use, or potential use, of the Internet as a marketing channel. How would it affect relationships with your existing channel to market?

Marketing Fundamentals

Feedback to activities

Activity 7.1

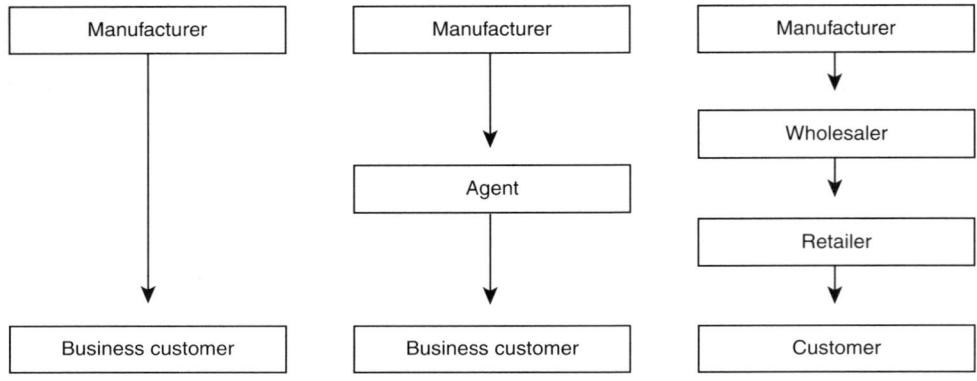

Activity 7.2

Farm – supermarket	Factors	Photocopier manufacturer – business
Farmer may use local market as a "broker" for goods.	**Where the market is and likely sales volume.**	Unlikely to sell large numbers of machines – need to have depots in all geographical regions.
Perishable – need to sell while fresh.	**Product characteristics.**	Heavy equipment.
Supermarket buying is very competitive.	**Competitor activity.**	Likely to use similar routes to market.
Low value items.	**Cost.**	High value, large items.
Essential – because of short product life.	**Reliability.**	Essential – because of need to supply in good repair.

Farm – supermarket	Factors	Photocopier manufacturer – business
Not an issue.	**Security issues.**	Medium importance.
Not applicable.	**Level of customer service involved.**	Installation, training, after-sales support.
Products must be fit for purpose and records kept to show "age".	**Legal issues.**	Products must be fit for purpose. Contracts drawn up showing terms and conditions.

Activity 7.3

You may have identified the following points:

- The main additional benefit is convenience.
- The language used on the sites deliberately recreates the shopping experience, e.g. basket, trolley, checkout, special offers, aisles, shelves.
- They use words such as "hand pick" to imply that they take as much care as you would if you were there choosing the goods.
- They reassure you about site security.
- Value is added through provision of recipe ideas, healthy eating features etc.

Session 8

Promotion

Introduction

This Session explores the various tools that combine to form the promotional mix. It looks at the advantages and disadvantages of each of these tools, and how they can be effectively co-ordinated to communicate with target audiences. Communicating with customers is such an important area of marketing that it is covered much more fully in the Customer Communications module at this level of study. The emphasis in this Session is to show the key components of the promotional mix and how it integrates with the overall marketing mix.

LEARNING OUTCOMES

At the end of this Session you will be able to:

- Describe the extensive range of tools that comprise the marketing communications mix, and examine the factors that contribute to its development and implementation.

Introduction to the promotional mix

The promotional mix is made up of advertising, public relations, sales promotion and personal selling. These four methods include many tools, some of which are covered below.

Advertising

This includes TV, radio, press, cinema, outdoor (billboard) and Internet "banner" advertising. All of these can be used to **D**ifferentiate a product or service, **R**emind customers of the benefits of a product or service, **I**nform or educate potential customers who may be going through the information search phase of the buying process, or to **P**ersuade them to buy.

Remember **DRIP**, for the objectives that promotional tools can be used to meet.

More and more TV adverts are now also directing audiences to web sites to obtain even more information. Advertising can be used not only to promote awareness of a product or service around its launch, but also to keep reminding the public of its existence during the year. It can also help to balance the affects of negative publicity.

Public relations

Companies receive an enormous amount of publicity. However, much of it can be negative in nature. Public relations is defined as 'a planned and sustained effort to establish and maintain goodwill between an organisation and its publics'. Public relations can be used to reinforce advertising in creating awareness, and through a planned effort, it can be used to develop stronger links with the press, so that any negative coverage can be minimised. Regional events and school visits are examples of activities that can be used to promote a positive image to a younger target audience.

Sales promotion

This involves offering inducements or incentives to customers. In the case of visiting a tourist attraction for example, reduced price tickets might be offered on a group basis, because of the volume of sales. Similar offers might be made at quieter times to increase throughput. Families would be less likely to visit during school time, so incentives could be offered to other groups to encourage them to visit during this period.

A sales promotion is designed to increase sales at the time of the promotion, and is not aimed at achieving long-term customer loyalty.

Most High Street retailers rely on customers returning to their stores to make repeat purchases. As consumers increasingly shopped around in the '90s, many supermarkets introduced loyalty cards to encourage customers to spend more money with them. Most cards work on a points system – the more you buy the more points you earn. The points can be exchanged for other goods and services or money-off vouchers. In addition, supermarkets promote certain products by offering extra points if they are purchased.

Organisations can use these loyalty cards to build databases of information about their customers and their preferences, in order to target promotions more effectively. Information can be gathered in a number of other ways, such as customer satisfaction surveys following purchases and via customer records of individual purchases. For example, car dealerships may store information for each customer on the date and nature of their last purchase, their age, social grouping and family status, in order to target those customers most likely to buy when they launch a new model.

It is increasingly important for the "bricks and mortar" retailers to keep in touch with their customers and their changing requirements, because there are so many other opportunities to purchase elsewhere. Internet shopping is growing in popularity as consumers become more confident about security and willing to use new technology. Many Christmas shoppers will e-shop this year to avoid the crowds and because they expect to find bargains on the Internet.

Personal selling

This involves the use of a sales force to promote products and services, usually on a one-to-one basis. This is more appropriate for selling in a business-to-business environment, or in the sale of services such as financial products. Here the product/service is complex in nature, and needs careful explanation. The communication message can then be personalised immediately to the buyer's need.

Factors which influence the selection of the most suitable tools include:

Company resources

TV advertising, for example, is very expensive, and for smaller companies it may not be a realistic option. Smaller companies tend to use direct mail and more localised campaigns, and increasingly the Internet.

Promotional objectives

Are you looking to differentiate your product or service from that offered by the competition? Consumer marketers may use TV advertising to achieve this, particularly if there is a large audience to reach. Business-to-business marketers are more likely to use personal selling to get their message across.

How carefully the message needs to be controlled or managed

The relative importance of an exact message being communicated and received by an audience will impact on the selection of the promotional tool. Advertising and sales promotion are very controllable, whereas with public relations there is less control over what the media actually print, and a sales force will personalise the message to each customer.

The level of credibility you want your audience to perceive

Public relations tends to communicate the most credibility, as there is often an objective outsider involved in the communication. The public often perceive this objective input as far more credible.

The nature of the target audience, and where it is

Large, consumer markets, that are spread internationally, are more suited to the use of mass communications such as advertising. Business-to-business audiences usually have complex Decision-Making Units, and will usually be best targeted through personal selling.

Promotional tools are rarely used in isolation. It is important that the mix of tools selected to communicate a standard message to an audience does so clearly, and that they do not contradict one another.

Activity 8.1

Which promotional tools do you think would be most appropriate for the following scenarios?

1. The launch of a new ice cream product within the UK.

2. Selling heavy plant and machinery to engineering companies in your home market.

3. Selling books to consumers.

Buying behaviour and the promotional mix

The consumer buyer decision process involves five stages, as shown below.

Problem recognition – a need is recognised.

Information search – the search for information about suitable products or services to satisfy that need is conducted.

Evaluation of alternatives – when information has been gathered, there may be several options open to the potential customer. They will have their own criteria for selecting one of these options.

Purchase decision – the purchase takes place (or the prospective customer decides not to proceed).

Post-purchase evaluation – the buyer decides whether the product met the level of satisfaction of their needs that they anticipated.

Promotional tools play a part at each stage of this process. Sometimes they prompt the recognition of a need. At other times they need to provide a suitable level of information to help the customer select a product. Potential purchasers may consult family and friends as part of their information search or evaluation process – promotion can help by reminding these people of the benefits your product offers. Advertising that emphasises the difference between your product and that of a competitor may help in the evaluation of alternatives, and prompt a purchase decision. In the post-purchase phase, customers may look to the promotion of a product to help them convince themselves that they made the right decision.

The factors that can influence the buying decision process are categorised as **personal** influences, **psychological** influences and **social** influences.

Let's use a car purchase to illustrate how some of these influences work.

Purchasing a car involves extensive decision making, as it is an expensive investment that is made infrequently. It is a high-involvement purchase, and so the potential customer will spend a lot of time and energy researching the purchase before making their final decision.

The pricing issue within the car industry will impact on the final purchase decision, not only with regard to which manufacturer is chosen, but whether the purchase is made in the UK or from the EU. It has been shown that prices for many new cars in the UK are inexplicably higher than in the rest of the EU. However, as this issue affects the pricing of cars from all manufacturers it will not make such a difference between brands, unless one manufacturer differentiates itself by adopting a lower pricing policy, and if price is the main consideration for the purchaser. All of this information needs to be communicated and made easily accessible to the potential buyer.

Other factors that impact on the decision as to whether to buy a car are:

- Demographic factors, in particular, age, sex, income and family life cycle.

- Situational factors. For example, if the buyer has just started a new job and needs a car to travel to work, this may put pressure on them to buy earlier, with a much shorter information search.

- Psychological factors, such as how the manufacturer is perceived in terms of what is most important to the buyer, e.g. safety or self-image. Previous experience of a particular manufacturer will also have an influence in this category.

- Social influences include the influence of the family, other reference groups (such as friends or work colleagues), and social class.

Marketers need to understand how these factors influence buyers so that they can shape their promotional offering to meet customers' needs.

Business-to-business customers also go through a buying decision process, whose stages are very similar to those made by consumers. The Internet has improved the buying process for Small to Medium-sized Enterprises (SMEs) as is illustrated in the following example.

Recognition of problem – this may be the recognition of a new purchase need, or a re-buy situation.

Development of product specifications to solve problem – the end-users of the product, together with technical specialists, will work to develop an appropriate specification. The Internet may have helped the company identify new ideas regarding product usage, as it makes information more accessible to smaller companies.

Search for products and suppliers – this is where the Internet can really help. Previously, companies may have been limited to directories and local companies to find suppliers. Now companies not only have the ability to search much wider, but they can use reverse auctions to request tenders.

Evaluate products and suppliers relative to specifications – a short list of suppliers and products are evaluated against criteria previously set by the company, or tenders are considered and responded to.

Select and order most appropriate products – preference may be given to those who have online purchase facilities.

Evaluate product and supplier performance – company considers whether the purchase was the best one and whether it worked. Because their choice has broadened, power now lies with them as the buyer, and should they choose to, they could switch supplier much more easily.

Companies wishing to target SMEs need to ensure that their web sites communicate appropriate benefits for SMEs, to meet the needs of organisations looking to buy this way. Depending on the complexity of the product or service offered, they may combine e-promotion with advertising in trade magazines (or on trade portals) and personal selling.

Activity 8.2

DRIP is often used as a mnemonic to illustrate the different purposes advertising might be used for. Consider the consumer buying process and prepare notes for a meeting at which you have been asked to talk about how promotion can be used to help move the customer through the decision-making process.

New media

In recent years, the development of a variety of new media has expanded the opportunities open to marketers when communicating with the various audiences they wish to target. The development of relationship marketing has already led to improvements in communication between a company and its suppliers, its staff and its customers. It is also responsible for creating further demands and expectations, both within companies and by customers, for further benefits through communication.

These new media include the Internet, mobile phones, Direct Response TV (DRTV), and ambient media (such as advertising on supermarket trolleys, beer mats, the outside of taxis and even the Houses of Parliament once!).

Some of the most common types of electronic media and terms are explained below.

Banner ads

A banner ad is usually a rectangular advertisement on a web site that is "hot linked" to the advertiser's site. It offers the Internet user the opportunity to "click through" to see information that the advertiser wants to make available to the web user on its own web site. It is therefore important to place banner ads on sites that you know are already attracting your target audience. The banner can be static or animated (to attract attention).

Banner ads can be used for two main purposes. They can help increase awareness of the company, brand or product, as all visitors to the host page will see it either consciously or subconsciously (Amazon.com advertised extensively on the Internet to raise awareness of their brand). They can also attract more visitors to the actual web site, so more information can be provided for them. This is what most advertisers hope will happen.

They can also be used by the owner of the site on which the ad is placed as a way of calculating the value of their site. Banner ads are usually charged on a "click through" rate – how many visitors actually click on the ad and visit the advertisers web site. This can be measured by the host and then charged to the advertiser.

Like all elements of the promotional mix, banner or online advertising needs to work with the other elements to be effective. Like off-line advertising, it also needs to be renewed and updated so that viewers are less likely to get used to seeing it and end up ignoring it. This is being referred to as "banner blindness".

Ideal locations for banner ads include portals, news services and relevant special interest sites. The more effective ads may carry incentives for the visitor to click through. For example, competitions or special offers may be designed differently for different sites, and may be located to "appear" when the visitor searches for an appropriate keyword.

Communities

A group of web users with similar interests who are attracted back to a particular site because it allows them to interact with one another.

Extranets

An extension of an Intranet to specialist groups of users, such as suppliers. Usually password protected.

Interstitials

"Pop-up" windows containing advertisements.

Intranets
A network within a company giving staff access to essential information.

Opt-in emails
Only customers that have explicitly requested information are contacted by email.

Portals
A web site that provides a gateway to information on the Internet through directories, search engines and personalised news via email or on a site.

Activity 8.3

Explain how the following tools can be used to communicate with the audiences of an organisation:

1. Internet.
2. Extranet.
3. Intranet.

Packaging's role in promotion

Packaging is said to fulfil four main functions – protection, promotion, provision of information and convenience.

It has been called "the silent salesman", as, particularly for Fast Moving Consumer Goods (FMCG), packaging is the only way of communicating brand image on the supermarket shelf.

For example, a company making healthy food products, such as Whole Earth, might use packaging to promote the brand and attract the eye. When Whole Earth's products were sold through specialist shops, it was competing directly with similar foods. Now that it is on supermarket shelves it faces indirect competition from "non-health" foods and other goods.

Packaging also fulfils a communication role in the provision of information. Many countries (including the UK) have legislation that states that certain information must be placed on the packaging of foodstuffs, for example the ingredients. Whole

Earth will want to communicate the way in which its brand is differentiated against competitors, i.e. natural ingredients, organically grown.

Activity 8.4

Your Marketing Manager has asked you to obtain some quotes for repackaging your product, following a major restyle and the development of a new logo. You have obtained the following information.

Fantasy Design & Co.   Labels – 43p each.
Folders – £1,200 per 5,000.
Outer boxes (flat pack printed) – £1.03 each.

Your current supplier. A good relationship exists, but delivery has been questionable once or twice in the last year.

Moon & Stars Printing Ltd.   Labels – 41p each.
Folders – £1,250 per 5,000.
Outer boxes (flat pack printed) – £1.00 each.

A local company (established ten years), not yet tested on any print job.

Natty Graphics Partnership   Labels – 39p each.
Folders – £1,000 per 5,000.
Outer boxes (flat pack printed) – £0.99 each.

This is a new start-up company, aggressively looking for business.

Your initial order will be for 50,000 labels, 15,000 folders, and 5,000 outer boxes.

1. Which quote is the cheapest?

2. What other factors would you take into account in reaching your decision?

3. What will you recommend to your Manager?

Case Study – Pride and prejudice

They've been the butt of endless jokes for as long as people can remember, but as the winners of two top awards at this year's Marketing Effectiveness Awards, it looks like Skoda might have the last laugh. By Jill Wyatt.

At the end of the '90s, despite wide acknowledgement in the UK motoring press that Skoda cars had improved beyond recognition, deep-rooted brand prejudice among consumers remained. But that was before Chris Hawken became Skoda's Marketing Manager and introduced a radical marketing approach that has transformed the car manufacturers fortunes – an achievement recognised by two awards at the Marketing Week/CIM Effectiveness Awards 2000.

Question: 'Why have Skodas got heated rear windows?' Answer: 'To keep your hands warm when you're pushing them up a hill.' No other car manufacturer has been the butt of so many jokes, but times have changed and so, finally, have public perceptions of Skoda.

This year's radical marketing campaign won Skoda the Grand Prix in the Marketing Week/CIM Effectiveness Awards 2000 and its Marketing Manager, Chris Hawken, the title of Marketer of the Year.

In December 1998, Hawken was invited to move from his role as Fleet Marketing Manager for Volkswagen to Marketing Manager for its subsidiary Skoda. 'Shortly afterwards I went on holiday to France with a group of friends from university,' he says. 'When I announced my intended career move to them, they descended into hysterical laughter – a fairly predictable response. However, I knew that I was taking on a real job, marketing a fantastic product, with huge customer loyalty and a strong dealer network. Naturally I also recognised the challenge that deep-rooted brand prejudice would pose.'

Despite acknowledgement in the motoring press over recent years that the quality of Skoda cars had improved beyond recognition, to the vast majority of drivers the brand was still a joke. Qualitative and quantitative research by Quadrangle and Millward Brown had repeatedly shown that the majority of people would not consider a Skoda when buying a new car. 'I decided that it was time to stop the research and do something about what it told us,' says Hawken.

Hawken recognised that one of the problems with Skoda's advertising was the pan-European approach it had adopted. 'All advertising is devised centrally by the Grey agency,' he explains. 'This is fine if you have a strong brand that means the same thing in all countries, but that wasn't the case with Skoda. There was a failure to recognise that the brand meant something different in most western European countries, and that the UK had a specific problem to address.'

'I also felt that the advertising wasn't talking to people. It made the presumption that people were interested in the product and did nothing to challenge brand prejudice. The reality was that the buying public didn't care whether the product was good – they still wouldn't be seen dead in a Skoda!'

An unhappy market

By mid-1999, Hawken admits he was getting increasingly desperate. 'I wanted a big brand campaign, ready to deliver a positive advertising message on the new Fabia and time was ticking by,' he says.

Furthermore, as if the task of turning Skoda round wasn't big enough, the market situation did not bode well either. The advertising budget available for the Fabia was £4.5 million. This was £2.7 million less than had been devoted to Skoda's previous model launch two years before. By contrast, in 1999 Toyota had spent £9 million on the Yaris launch, while Renault spent £17 million on the relaunched Clio (Source: MMS).

Another potential stumbling block was the fact that unlike Skodas in the past, the Fabia was not a budget car. In fact, the starting price was higher than that for a Vauxhall Corsa, and on a par with mainstream competitors.

Despite resistance from his colleagues in the Czech Republic, Hawken invited two new agencies to put together a creative proposition designed 'to really hit the mark'. Advertising agency Fallon was the clear winner.

The advertising campaign devised by the agency used the copy line 'It's a Skoda. Honest.', and focused on the gap between people's expectations of a Skoda and the reality, using self-deprecating humour to win the right to gain consumers' re-evaluation. After Fallon's presentation in September, the advertising was put to the test in research. With the agency's approach totally vindicated, the ads were shot, and the £2.85 million TV campaign ran for five weeks in early Spring 2000. It was supported by a £600,000 poster campaign and a £274,000 spend in the colour press.

The new advertising was combined with more basic forms of marketing, including mystery shopping, training retail staff, and product placement in high-profile locations. Integrated PR was used to extend and amplify the message, and editorial in leading national press, TV and radio both confirmed the power of the campaign and contributed to its momentum.

Source: Extract from 'Pride and prejudice', *Marketing Business*, December/January 2001.

Questions

1. What was the challenge faced by Skoda's new Marketing Manager?
2. What was the message communicated by the new campaign?
3. List the full range of promotional tools used in the new campaign.

SUMMARY OF KEY POINTS

In this Session we have explored all aspects of the promotional mix, and covered the following key points:

- The promotional mix includes advertising, sales promotion, PR, and personal selling.
- Each promotional tool has advantages and disadvantages, which affect their suitability for use in specific situations.
- The marketer needs to select appropriate media for its audience, its message and its available resources.
- New media have expanded the options available to the marketer.
- Buyer behaviour influences the type of communication necessary at various stages of the buying decision process.

Improving and developing own learning

The following projects are designed to help you develop your knowledge and skills further, by carrying out some research yourself. Feedback is not provided for this type of learning because there are no "answers" to be found, but you may wish to discuss your findings with colleagues and fellow students.

Project A

Select one of your products or services and identify the way the promotional mix is made up.

Project B

Look at one of your company's advertisements, or one you select from the press or TV. Identify the target audience, the message being communicated and the general objective of the ad.

Project C

Find out how your organisation is using electronic media to communicate with its target audiences.

Feedback to activities

Activity 8.1

1. Pre-launch PR, TV ads and magazines.
   In-store promotion with "tasting" and sales promotion vouchers.
   Continuation of advertising campaign.

2. Trade journals, web site, personal selling.

3. Direct mail, web site, advertising to retailers.

Activity 8.2

Meeting notes

Promotion's role in moving the buyer through their decision process

1. Consumer buying process:
    i) Problem recognition.
    ii) Information search.

iii) Evaluation of alternatives.

iv) Purchase decision.

v) Post-purchase evaluation.

2. i) Advertising can help consumer awareness and highlight "problems". Care must be taken not to "create" a need.

   ii) Advertising, web site, e-newsletters, technical specifications, and information sheets/packs linked to benefits of products.

   iii) Opinion leaders/formers often consulted at this stage. We need to ensure that we have provided information targeted at, or using this group. PR in technical or specialist magazines, exhibitions, etc.

   iv) "Call to action" in promotional material. Sales promotion can be used at this stage.

   v) Inclusion of guarantees, after-sales support, warranties, and return policies in easily understandable and accessible formats.

Activity 8.3

1. Internet – customers and potential customers. Not only through our own web site but also through ads/information on related sites, portals etc. Corporate information provided for key stakeholders.

2. Extranet – suppliers and key customers. Often password protected – prices, policies, terms, etc.

3. Intranet – staff. Key information about progress to plans, new policies.

Activity 8.4

1. Natty Graphics.

2. Existing supplier is tried and tested, and may be able to negotiate a discount. Local supplier is well established, but untried. New company has little experience and prices may rise in the near future.

3. Try to negotiate a discount with the existing supplier. If this is not possible, recommend splitting the order between the existing supplier and Moon & Stars Printing Ltd.

Session 9

Service marketing

Introduction

This Session introduces the main differences between products and services, and the way in which the extended marketing mix can help deal with these differences. It also looks at the contribution of customer service in meeting customer needs in the product mix as well as the service mix.

> **LEARNING OUTCOMES**
>
> At the end of this Session you will be able to:
>
> - Explain the importance of people in marketing, and in particular appreciate the contribution staff make to effective service delivery.
> - Explain the importance of service in satisfying customer requirements, and identify the factors that contribute to the delivery of service quality.

The role of people in the marketing mix

Services differ from products in that they are consumed at the point of delivery. Therefore, the people element means that each service, such as financial advice, a haircut or eye examination, will be similar but not exactly the same each time. In contrast, products are manufactured under controlled conditions so that each tin of baked beans, washing machine or copy of a best-selling novel will be exactly the same each time.

The differences between products and services are:

Intangibility

A service cannot be touched and inspected in the same way a product can, so the judgement of quality is subjective. It is based on experience and personal feelings. For one person the attention received from a restaurant waiter will make the occasion special, whilst another person may find it overwhelming and intrusive.

Inseparability

The consumer must be present (or logged on if accessing an electronic service, such as Internet banking), otherwise there is no requirement for the service. The

Internet has increased the ability of organisations to provide services for consumers at times and places that are convenient for them (hence the rise in companies providing "e" services). However, when things go wrong the personal touch is still appreciated by consumers, and remains a significant reason why consumers do not purchase complex products, such as some financial services, via the Internet.

Heterogeneity

As previously mentioned, standardisation is difficult to achieve in services as the delivery may vary each time.

Perishability

Services cannot be stored. Unlike manufacturers who can plan for busy periods by building up stock, service providers need to be able to cope with peak demand at that time or they will "lose the sale".

Ownership

Customers do not own a service in the same way as they can permanently own a product. Payment is for a temporary ownership during use, for example the hire of a tennis court or taxi service.

From these characteristics of services it can be appreciated that there are certain problems related to the marketing of services that do not apply to the marketing of products.

Unlike products, a service cannot be seen and so is difficult to promote. The consumer benefits from the effects of the service and the enjoyment of the experience, rather than the permanent ownership of a tangible object. Therefore, the marketer needs to identify what these benefits are when advertising services and planning sales promotions. For example, a taxi firm might emphasise reliability and speed of response.

When marketing services it is common practice to promote the skill and expertise of the personnel providing the service, and the quality aspects of that service – speed, convenience etc. A solicitors' practice would include qualifications on the nameplate outside, so potential customers can see how well qualified they are to provide the service.

Testimony from previous clients is also used to gain client confidence and persuade them to try the service, but permission is required from the original source. This is similar to the marketing of products where recommendations might be used.

It is just as important to get the right mix when marketing services as it is for products. McDonald's would not satisfy customers if they were kept waiting for their meals, despite the friendly service and comfortable chairs. Quality of service is just as important as product quality.

> **Activity 9.1**
>
> Explain the terms intangibility, inseparability, heterogeneity, perishability and ownership when linked to a visit to the cinema. Next time you visit the cinema, make a note of any "people" skills that might be useful in your workplace.

Customer relationship management

Customer Relationship Management (CRM) is just one way of delivering customer care. Marketing today is more than just acquiring new customers – the "traditional" view of marketing. Since the early 1990s when the concept of CRM was developed, marketing has been just as much about retaining existing customers and generating high levels of repeat business. CRM aims not only to retain customers, but also to get customers to recommend your goods and services because they are so pleased with the way they have been treated.

What does CRM mean? It means different things to different people.

- To the **customer** it means that the company's representatives who talk to you know who you are, and have information at their fingertips, such as what you have bought in the past, what current orders remain unfulfilled and when delivery is due. It may also mean expectations of financial and other benefits.

- To the **company** it means higher levels of business with the same customers, and therefore lower marketing costs.

- To the **IT department** in the company it means large and complex information systems, capable of updating and delivering all relevant customer information to customer-facing staff.

For CRM to work, the company has to keep potentially large amounts of information about its customers. Naturally, it will want to pay most attention to its most profitable customers, often (but not always) those who spend most. This implies identifying and differentiating between customer groups. For example, supermarkets offer about 1% discount to cardholders, in return for the right to obtain personal information about their buying behaviour. However, not all customers carry store cards, so CRM recognises that not every customer participates in every scheme.

Will these schemes discourage non-cardholders and infrequent users from shopping in these stores? It might if price discounts were only available to cardholders. But the supermarkets use CRM as just one weapon in their marketing armoury, along with an array of discounts and promotions to appeal to other groups.

This highlights the importance of identifying different customer groups for a company's goods and services, and then using an appropriate customer care strategy. CRM's biggest contribution to business has been to focus companies on their relationships with customers over time, rather than just the sales transaction. CRM may be valuable, but is not appropriate for all businesses or all groups of customers.

> **Activity 9.2**
>
> You work for a provider of telecommunications equipment to small businesses.
>
> List the information you might expect to keep on a customer database used to develop relationships with your customers.
>
> Who should be notified of the purpose for which you store this data (for legal reasons)?

Service marketing in action

Services differ from products in that they are intangible, perishable, heterogeneous and inseparable. They cannot be touched, smelled or tasted in the same way as products can, and they rely heavily on the people involved in their delivery for their quality. In order to deal with these differences, they not only use the traditional 4 Ps of Product, Price, Promotion and Place, but also the Ps of People, Process and Physical Evidence.

Service marketing

Let's consider the services offered both on and off-line by banks as an example.

People – banks with physical branches can make a real difference in this area. Customers may be content in dealing on the Internet for most of their basic day-to-day transactions, but when they are considering something more complex, such as a pension, or more significant, such as a mortgage, they prefer to deal on a face-to-face basis.

Of course, it is essential that the staff involved are well trained, have excellent product knowledge, give good customer service and present a professional appearance.

Process – in terms of process, software that lets the bank down, and web sites that crash or cannot be accessed when customers need them, do not present a good image. In the case of a bank that already has branches, it needs to ensure that any technology-based service satisfies the customer expectations it has created with its physical presence.

For Internet-only banks looking to link to a bank with branches, there is a need to recognise that just having branches is not enough. The processes in place need to be customer focused, allowing customers to make appointments when they are free to attend, know that they will be seen promptly and dealt with efficiently, and feel confident that any necessary follow-up action will be carried out.

Physical evidence – bank branches have changed significantly over the past decade. Whilst many retain the "barrier" of the traditional counter for cash transactions, an increasing number have created open-plan banking halls, with staff the same side of the "barrier" as the customers, creating a friendlier atmosphere.

The colours and décor are also important, and need to reflect the same image as the logo and corporate communications. To add "physical evidence" of the Internet service, it would be useful to have screens accessible in the banking hall for customers to try or to see demonstrations.

Activity 9.3

Your local hairdresser has asked for your advice about marketing their service. Explain to them the importance of the People, Process and Physical Evidence elements of the marketing mix, with specific reference to their service.

The role of people in delivering service quality

Customers' perceptions of how well a service meets their expectations is referred to as service quality. It is difficult to ensure standardisation of performance because people are involved in the delivery of a service. However, there are certain steps an organisation can take to try and improve the quality of their service.

There are said to be four service quality factors:

Understanding customer expectations – it is very important that this is properly researched and not just assumed. Common forms of research undertaken are customer feedback forms, postal questionnaires and follow-up phone calls.

Service quality specifications – service specifications, or service standards, should be set with the aim of meeting and exceeding customer expectations. Ideally, they should be set and agreed with the agreement and involvement of all front-line staff responsible for their delivery. Examples include answering the phone within 3-4 rings, making eye contact with the customer, greeting the customer within 2 minutes of them entering the premises, etc.

Employee performance – once service standards are set, management must do all they can to ensure that staff are properly equipped to meet them on a consistent basis. Training is essential, and rewards linked to customer satisfaction rather than sales volume are also important.

Managing service expectations – finally, not only is it important to manage the staff delivering the service, but also to set customer expectations appropriately at the outset of the relationship. Marketers must take care not to over-promise in communications. Customers are less likely to be disappointed if expectations are set appropriately.

Case Study – Marketing meets the law

Brian Jenner gives an overview of the problems facing marketers who work in the legal profession.

Law firms are now global businesses, facing constant change. They pay high wages for good marketing staff and have plenty of funds to pursue ideas. The Law Society only allowed the profession to advertise in the early 80s, so there is still room for innovative thinking. It's a dream challenge for an ambitious marketing professional, with only one drawback. You have to work with lawyers.

That would be fine if lawyers were businessmen, with a sharp eye for the balance sheet and a keen understanding of the changing demands of the marketplace. But that is not the case. They like to see themselves as Jedi knights in pin-stripe suits, quasi-academics who are sought out for their mental agility and wise counsel. Marketing people remind them of the prosaic reality that they are merely selling a service like a plumber or an estate agent. It is a tribute to the persistence of marketing professionals that after a recent business strategy presentation, a barrister in chambers agreed that the ideas were 'repulsive but necessary'. It has been a constant struggle to persuade solicitors and barristers that their practices must evolve, and that they can't solve the problems by themselves.

Marketers who are familiar with clearly-defined management structures can find the organisation of law firms confusing, and indeed infuriating. Traditionally, solicitors' firms are partnerships. This means that the practice is owned by a group of individuals, and everyone likes to have their say. So, even if a decision is approved by the managing partner, other partners (who have clout because of their reputation or clients) can refuse to co-operate.

Barristers' chambers may share facilities, but they don't share profits. They don't operate as a company but as a group of individuals. The marketer has got to understand these unusual structures, and develop a way of adapting a professional marketing agenda to an arcane way of life.

Making marketing respectable

Lawyers have a perception that marketing is somehow not a respectable pastime. 'Marketing and selling are typically seen as activities which lack integrity,' says Kim Tasso, an independent consultant. For this reason, lawyers like to see the marketing department as a hole in the bucket. Marketers may produce glossy brochures, put on a few parties, have a slightly better dress sense, but what do they actually contribute to the bottom line?

Marketers in turn have a habit of posing awkward questions to lawyers, like, 'Is this profitable?' or 'Can I see the business plan?', which is greeted with blank incomprehension. Sadly, lawyers find it very hard to respect anyone who hasn't got a legal training, so any suggestions from marketing on the overall business strategy tends to provoke furrowed brows, implying 'Stick to the Christmas card list, thank you very much'.

'The market is ever more competitive, and if lawyers want the high value work, they are going to have to compete for it,' says Richard Haynes, from Haynes Consulting in Warwick, which has been advising law firms for the past eight years.

He sees much improvement in the attitude of solicitors firms and, more recently, a growing receptiveness from barristers' chambers. 'When you convince solicitors that they have to meet a new client on average about six times before getting any work, they realise they can't just sit at their desks all day waiting for it to come to them'.

Haynes has been introducing a strategy called "spark and torch", which encourages the clerks in barristers' chambers to refocus their roles. The clerk, by tradition, brings in the work. However, rather than waiting for solicitors to call them, the "spark and torch" method means that the clerks take a more proactive attitude to approaching solicitors who might only use them a little, to encourage them to use them much more. Then the "torch" side of the strategy trains barristers to use their networking skills in social situations to build potential client relationships. 'The clerks are receptive,' says Haynes, 'and "pockets" of barristers are taking it on board.'

Measuring the bottom line

One of the main problems for marketers, once installed, is the difficulty in measuring their contribution to the firm. In this respect, accountancy firms are three to five years ahead of law firms. They have devised the concept of a marketing audit. This provides a framework to analyse the organisation's performance. Law firms are slowly absorbing these principles, and gradually accepting the need for a "marketing plan".

Solicitors traditionally get all their work from referrals. Some solicitor firms like Slaughter & May, one of the top five, still do not officially have a marketing department. They maintain the disdainful attitude that they get work through the "recommendation of their clients".

Given the problems facing legal marketers, it is encouraging to see new marketing ideas. For example, Rowe and Maw, a medium-sized City firm, has just launched an advertising campaign on the London Underground. Previously, firms have taken hoardings to launch new offices and for recruitment advertising, but this is the first time it has been tried for "brand building".

'This is part of an ongoing campaign that started three years ago in the FT,' says Rowe & Maw's Marketing Director, Chris Pullen. 'The adverts have been criticised for being too unfocused, but the legal market now has clear divisions, and we were aware that our name was not well known. We've had a good response from clients.' Chris Pullen is lucky. In an area where staff turnover is high, he has managed to stay in the job for eight years and win the confidence of the lawyers. Consequently, the firm and his Department are now growing steadily.

Accountancy firms are ahead of lawyers in other areas. They have introduced telemarketing, which means people go through the database, phoning potential clients, determining their needs, and then arranging for a partner to sell, for example, an audit, as a "tangible, wrapped product". Legal services are slightly more difficult to sell in this way, but in theory, this will come.

Technology also threatens to radically change the way law firms do their business. Linklaters & Alliance launched their Blue Flag system, a packaged, legal service delivered by the Internet in 1996. It started by supplying European law on cross-border regulations for investment banks and global institutions. It has now been widened to other practice areas, including Asia-Pacific jurisdictions. 'It's a good name and the service has helped to raise our profile across the City and worldwide,' says Emma Hunter their Marketing Officer.

'All law firms now realise that having a web site is a key marketing tool. The web site is the mainstay of our marketing activity,' says Paula Allerton, Marketing Manager of niche insurance practice Davies Lavery. The introduction of case and practice management systems has also dramatically changed the way legal marketing is done. While the marketing database used to reside in the marketing department and information was dispersed, inaccurate and very difficult to capture, it is now possible to centralise data on accounting, time management and billing. It has removed the drudgery of inputting contact details and finding out information from others.

To date, professional services marketing has not been subject to the same cardinal rules as product marketing. However, as building relationships with clients has become much more important, legal marketers have suddenly found themselves at the cutting edge.

Firms have started to introduce client-care training for partners, fee-earners and support staff. Previously marketing staff had to limit their client contact to seminars and social events, but this is changing. The marketer has to keep urging lawyers to think ahead more than a few months, and to operate as a team, rather than individuals. 'The concept of client loyalty is well and truly dead. Lawyers know that if they are going to win and keep clients, they have to be more proactive,' says the head of business development at a leading City firm.

Source: Extract from 'Marketing meets the Law', *Marketing Business*, December/January 2000.

Marketing Fundamentals

> **Questions**
>
> 1. Explain how the "people" element of the marketing mix can be used effectively for legal firms.
>
> 2. What promotional activity can you identify from the Case Study?
>
> 3. How might marketing audits help the legal firms that have started to market their practices?

> ## SUMMARY OF KEY POINTS
>
> In this Session we have explored the differences between products and services, and how the marketer can accommodate these differences. We have also covered the following key points:
>
> - The main differences between products and services are intangibility, inseparability, heterogeneity, perishability and ownership.
>
> - These differences can be accommodated by marketers through the extended marketing mix.
>
> - The additional 3 Ps in the extended marketing mix are People, Process and Physical Evidence.
>
> - Customer Relationship Management (CRM) is one way of delivering quality customer service.

Improving and developing own learning

The following projects are designed to help you develop your knowledge and skills further, by carrying out some research yourself. Feedback is not provided for this type of learning because there are no "answers" to be found, but you may wish to discuss your findings with colleagues and fellow students.

> **Project A**
>
> The extended marketing mix can be used in the marketing of products as well as services. Find out to what extent the additional 3Ps are relevant to marketing within your company or one you know well.

Service marketing

> **Project B**
>
> Next time you use a service such as a visit to your bank, or to the hairdressers, identify how they use the additional 3 Ps to market their service.

> **Project C**
>
> Identify how your college or business school uses the extended marketing mix to market its services to you.

Feedback to activities

Activity 9.1

Intangibility – the film cannot be touched, or taken away. Tickets, reviews etc. provide some tangibility.

Inseparability – consumes at the time of the showing. You need to be there to experience the big screen, atmosphere etc.

Heterogeneity – experiences with staff will invariably vary. Although the film will be the same each time, the audience watching will change with each showing, possibly affecting your enjoyment, e.g. screaming kids or noisy teenagers.

Perishability – once the film has started tickets can no longer be sold.

Ownership – temporary "ownership" is taken for the time of the showing.

Activity 9.2

Typical information for inclusion would be:

Name of contact
Job title
Address
Telephone number
Email address
Fax number
Number of employees

Nature of business
Date of last contact
Date of last purchase
Value of last purchase
Services used

The Data Protection Registrar should be notified of the purpose for which you hold customer data.

Activity 9.3

Examples may include the following:

People	Well trained, uniforms, diplomas displayed, all pleasant and smiling, good customer service.
Process	Computerised appointment system, records of customer history kept, telephone reminders before next appointment (if wanted).
Physical evidence	Clean and bright premises, comfortable seating while waiting, tidy waiting area, books and magazines available, relaxing environment, background music playing.

Session 10

ICT and monitoring marketing effectiveness

Introduction

This Session explores two very different, but important, aspects of marketing. The first is the way in which Information and Communications Technology (ICT) is changing and contributing to marketing processes. Secondly, it looks at the importance of measuring all aspects of marketing effectiveness, and considers the ways in which this can be achieved. Both of these aspects are very much at the forefront of today's marketing agenda, involving marketers at all levels of the profession.

> **LEARNING OUTCOMES**
>
> At the end of this Session you will be able to:
>
> - Examine the effects of Information and Communication Technology on the development and implementation of the marketing mix.
>
> - Explain the importance of measuring the effectiveness of the selected marketing effort, and instituting appropriate changes where necessary.

The role of ICT in implementing the marketing mix

In earlier Sessions of this module we explored the difficulties that exist in trying to put a customer-based philosophy into practice. The steps we identified included the following:

- Marketing strategy needs to be developed.
- The philosophy needs to be communicated clearly to all staff, so that a marketing-orientated culture can start to be developed.
- Customer needs must be determined and defined.
- Internal structures may need to be adapted to respond to customer needs.
- Products/services may need to be adapted.
- Resources will need to be invested in information systems.
- Customer care systems need to be put in place.

ICT and monitoring marketing effectiveness

- Effective mechanisms to measure and control performance to marketing plans and customer service standards must be put in place.

Developments in technology can help with the implementation of the marketing concept in several ways.

Marketing research and understanding the environment	The Internet can be used to gather market-intelligence and competitor information.
Communication with stakeholders	Intranets to communicate with staff, and Extranets to communicate with suppliers.
Understanding customers	Databases can be analysed to develop a better understanding of customer behaviour. For example what they buy, how often they buy, how much they buy, etc.
Growth of organisation	New markets can be reached via the Internet.
New distribution methods	E-commerce can be used to offer an alternative channel to get goods or services to the customer.
Service and promotion	Email and web sites can be used to improve customer care.

Drivers towards the use of e-marketing include:

- Increased sophistication and reducing price of technology.
- Growth in Internet use – 46% of households have Internet access in the UK, as of May 2002 (www.nua.ie – Nielsen NetRatings).
- Increased acceptance of using the Internet to make purchases.
- "Time poverty". Customers are increasingly busy with demanding working lives, and want to improve their lifestyle rather than spend time shopping. The

Internet can make organisations accessible 24/7 (24 hours a day, 7 days a week).

- Technology puts the customer in "control" of their shopping. They can quickly and easily search for the best prices for products and services, and will choose to stay on sites that entertain and offer added-value services.
- Reducing costs of access to the Internet.
- Ability to personalise interaction with customers much more cost effectively.
- The ability, for some organisations, to save money in the long-term through disintermediation (cutting out intermediaries from the supply chain).
- Competitive pressure – "if we don't, our competitors will".

Electronic media is still relatively new, and is changing constantly. Marketers need to continuously monitor and review any plans they make, and be prepared to respond quickly, as the real-time nature of the facility allows and dictates.

Aspects of ICT and their uses in specific areas of the mix, particularly promotion and distribution, have been covered in the appropriate Sessions.

Activity 10.1

Explain how the use of ICT could assist in the management of a customer-oriented culture within a business-to-business company.

The role of technology in changing the promotional mix

The traditional promotional mix includes advertising, public relations, sales promotion and personal selling. The use of technology, particularly in the call centre environment, has enabled companies to deal directly and more personally with customers, and to work far more cost effectively. The impact on each element of the promotional mix can be described as follows:

- Personal selling has always been the most expensive form of communication. However, it is very effective in business-to-business markets, where you are able to personalise and adapt the message instantly, according to the customer's needs. The use of telephone selling in customer acquisition frees the sales force to follow-up "qualified leads", and to develop relationships with valuable and profitable customers.

- Advertising through the Internet and digital TV has offered more targeted opportunities to reach customers and to gather information about customer behaviour. Direct Response TV (DRTV) has added an interactive element to advertising, so that responses can be gathered and acted upon.

- Sales promotions can now be targeted better through the use of databases. Web sites have been developed which offer discounts on purchases through the Internet, and also offer "downloads" which promote specific products or companies.

- Public relations – the Internet has proved an effective tool in communicating with both internal and external customers, and email has speeded up the transmission of press releases, particularly to the international press.

In addition to the above, Intranets and Extranets can be used to update information relevant to suppliers and staff almost instantly. This is particularly helpful to sales staff working remotely. In the past, it was uncomfortably common for a customer to give a salesperson information about their own company or products! This is much less likely now as a salesperson is able to link a laptop through a modem and phone line (sometimes a mobile phone line) and give the customer up-to-the-minute information whilst on the customer's premises.

As long as staff are given proper training and are familiar and comfortable with technology, then communication with customers should be improved through its use.

There are many ways in which technology has improved customer service in recent years. The following are just some examples.

- The Internet has improved access to information for customers, who can now choose when they want to search for information about products.

- Companies can access information in their customer databases that can then inform the development of products.

- Business-to-business customers can access product catalogues or price lists on their suppliers' Extranets or on CD-ROMs.

- Sophisticated databases and improved telephony systems have enabled call centres to build more personalised relationships with individual customers.

They can help by providing after-sales service support when the customer needs it on a one-to-one basis.

- This after-sales service support can be further improved through the Internet and email services. Internet pages of Frequently Asked Questions (FAQs) can be accessed directly by customers 24 hours a day, or email queries can be handled by a customer service department and answered promptly.
- Internal information held on computers can be searched, combined and analysed more easily than paper-based records.
- Customer complaints can be documented and analysed to improve customer service. Technology can also improve complaint handling, speeding up the process.

Activity 10.2

List the ways in which an airline might use a call centre to communicate with its customers and potential customers.

Monitoring marketing effectiveness

As was highlighted in Session 3, the final and very important stage of the marketing planning process is to review performance against objectives.

If the objectives are measurable, then the process is made much easier. The marketing manager is looking at overall performance to objectives, how effective and efficient activity has been, and how profitable activity has been.

Measuring the effectiveness of marketing is an important issue for the marketing profession. There is an old saying about a finance director who admits that advertising is only 50% effective – the problem is he'd love to know which 50%! In today's cost-conscious organisations, marketers are increasingly called upon to justify their expenditure on creating awareness and winning and retaining customers. In other words, justify the existence of the marketing department! As a profession, marketers must show how effective marketing really is and how it contributes to the bottom line.

There are various tools and techniques that can be used in this process, both of a quantitative and qualitative nature.

Quantitative measures

Sales analysis – comparison of sales volume and value against forecasts, against industry norms and against competitors.

Cost analysis – this breaks down the costs of the marketing activities to see what exactly each has achieved, and to see which have been the most effective.

The combination of sales and cost analysis can be carried out by product, by product line, by segment, by region, or by individual marketing effort.

Qualitative measures

Brand awareness – how much has awareness been improved through particular marketing activities.

Customer satisfaction levels – how well have these been maintained over the year.

A repeat of the detailed marketing audit as detailed in Session 2 also serves a purpose in reviewing marketing effectiveness.

Activity 10.3

Explain how an organisation might measure customer satisfaction.

Case Study – Pride and prejudice (continued)

This Case Study concludes the one used in Session 8, Promotion, and looks at the results of the Skoda campaign that was run.

The results were certainly dramatic. Prior to the campaign, the company's market share had never exceeded 1%. After it, not only were 61% of the target sales for the new Fabia reached in the first three months, but Skoda's total UK market share (by volume) had risen to 1.1%, with an all-time high of 1.3% share of the small car segment. Given the state of the car market, which was suffering its biggest sales crisis in decades due to the "Rip-Off Britain" furore and a dramatic fall in consumer confidence, these were significant achievements.

'The success of this marketing initiative has been above and beyond anything we could have expected,' says Rob Tracey, head of Skoda UK. 'It achieved more in three months than previous efforts had done in nine years. To us, this was testament to the power of brave and innovative brand marketing in overcoming ingrained consumer perceptions.'

Before campaign	After campaign
10,055 Skodas sold January-May 1999.	11,565 sold January-May 2000 (+15%).
Skoda had never had a waiting list.	1,500 Fabia's on order.
Research also highlighted a dramatic re-evaluation of the brand by consumers:	
54% of people agreed that Skodas are better than they used to be.	Increased 25% to 79%.
20% of people could imagine themselves driving a Skoda.	Increased to 33%.
60% would not consider buying a Skoda.	Best-ever figure of only 42% recorded.

Source: Millward Brown
Extract from 'Pride and prejudice', *Marketing Business*, December/January 2001.

Questions

1. Identify the three measures of marketing effectiveness that Skoda used in the Case Study.

2. Explain two further measures that they could have used.

3. Explain the difference between **quantitative** and **qualitative** measures, using examples from the Case Study to illustrate your answer.

SUMMARY OF KEY POINTS

In this Session we have explored the ways in which the use of ICT is changing the face of marketing, and also the importance of measuring the effectiveness of marketing activity. We have also covered the following key points:

- Developments in technology have enabled marketers to develop better relationships with their customers.
- ICT can be used at every stage of the planning process to help the organisation become more customer focused.
- Call centres provide a number of services to improve relationships, using information technology and other methods.
- The final stage of the marketing planning process is the establishment and use of systems to evaluate and control the plan.
- Both quantitative and qualitative measures of performance to the plan can be used.

Improving and developing own learning

The following projects are designed to help you develop your knowledge and skills further, by carrying out some research yourself. Feedback is not provided for this type of learning because there are no "answers" to be found, but you may wish to discuss your findings with colleagues and fellow students.

Project A

Identify two ways in which your organisation has changed the way it carries out its marketing as a direct result of using ICT within the past two years. What specific differences can you identify?

Project B

List the benefits that call centres can offer customer-focused organisations.

Marketing Fundamentals

> **Project C**
>
> Find out and write notes on three ways in which your organisation measures the effectiveness of its marketing activity.

Feedback to activities

Activity 10.1

Characteristics of the business-to-business sector:

- Large orders/few large customers.
- Prices involve higher level of negotiation.
- Personal selling heavily used.
- Profit objectives.

Need to understand environment and competitor activity.	The Internet can be used to gather market-intelligence and competitor information.
Communication with key customers and suppliers.	Extranets are useful here, to enable order tracking, check product prices and whether products are in stock.
Communication with employees.	Intranet can keep staff updated and involved.
Understanding customers.	Databases can be analysed to develop a better understanding of customer behaviour. For example what they buy, how often they buy, how much they buy, etc.
Growth of organisation.	New markets might be reached via the Internet.

New distribution methods.	E-commerce can be used to offer an alternative channel to get goods or services to the customer.
Service and promotion.	Email and web sites can be used to improve customer care.

Activity 10.2

Call centres might use:

Telephone.
Fax.
Email.
Text messages.

Activity 10.3

Analysis of complaints.

Proactive follow-up calls.

Proactive questionnaires – detailed versions by post, or a short form at the time of purchase.

Talking to front-line staff.

Session 11

Marketing in differing contexts

Introduction

So far this Companion has explored the fundamentals of marketing and its application mainly, but not exclusively, to consumer marketing. This is where marketing originally developed, so other sectors that started to use it had to learn how to adapt it to their needs. Other sectors have been using marketing successfully for a number of years and have developed their own variations of the models and techniques discussed so far.

This Session considers how the marketing mix is adapted for some of these other business sectors and settings. It looks specifically at business-to-business marketing, not-for-profit marketing and marketing to Small to Medium-sized Enterprises (SMEs), and how their different characteristics impact on marketing activity. Each of these "contexts", as we shall see, affect the importance of certain marketing decisions, the composition of the marketing mix, and the tools and techniques used to arrive at an effective marketing mix.

> ### LEARNING OUTCOMES
> At the end of this Session you will be able to:
>
> - Explain the importance of contextual settings in influencing the selection of, and emphasis given to, marketing mix tools.
>
> - Explain differences in the characteristics of various types of marketing context (FMCG, business to business, non-profit, SMEs), and their impact on marketing mix decisions.
>
> - Compare and contrast the marketing activities of organisations that operate and compete in different contextual settings.

The effect of different contexts on the marketing mix

The marketing mix has already been covered in Sessions 5-9, and we learnt in Session 5 how the mix can be adapted depending on the stage reached in the product life cycle. In Session 9, we saw how the mix can be adjusted further to deal with the specific characteristics of services and their differences from more tangible products. We have also seen, in Session 8, that buyer behaviour differs between consumer markets and business-to-business markets.

In this Session we will look in more depth at adaptations of the marketing mix, and how these apply to Small to Medium-sized Enterprises (SMEs), not-for-profit and business-to-business organisations. In Session 12 this will be extended still further to cover marketing in international contexts and the virtual environment.

SME marketing

SMEs are usually limited in their growth opportunities by financial constraints, and tend to start off as more marketing oriented than most. The owner, or just a few staff, get to know their customers personally, and regular dialogue with them helps the company keep pace with customers' changing needs. With just a few key customers, and the owner's active involvement with the customers, the company can very quickly adapt the product or service, or adjust the price, because one person, the owner, usually makes the decisions.

Distribution strategies are kept simple, and promotion tends to be undertaken on an "all we can afford" basis.

As the organisation grows, the owner can no longer do all the sales and marketing themselves, so therefore recruits one or more sales staff. Because the initial marketing approach was informal, and often unplanned, the organisation thinks it is still very customer focused. But it is often a sales-driven organisation that emerges, driven by short-term targets rather than a marketing orientation.

Due to their often smaller resources, SMEs need to tailor the marketing mix specifically to make the most of their strengths or weaknesses.

Product

This can change from an initially very flexible approach to customising the product, to one where it is assumed that communicating the benefits of the product to customers is adopting a customer focus. Small businesses can often succeed by finding a market niche, through which they can differentiate themselves from larger competitors.

Price

If a small business is trying to sell to large buyers, it may be more difficult to convince them of their reliability and financial stability. Clear pricing structures based on what the market will stand will help this process.

Place

Many SMEs deal directly with their customers, only taking on new channels to market when they have become established. Considerations include what products you offer, what channels your competitors use, and how the costs of each channel will impact on your prices.

Promotion

This is likely to be limited by the amount of budget available, and the owner's approach to setting the budget. If an "objective and task" approach to setting the promotional budget can be taken, then a more co-ordinated promotional plan is likely to be achieved. It is still unlikely that TV advertising will be used however, because of the high costs involved.

The basic principles of Fast Moving Consumer Goods (FMCG) or business-to-business marketing will apply to the SME, depending on its target market.

Activity 11.1
Complete the following table with a suggested marketing mix for a small business marketing hand-made cards and gifts.

Product	
Price	
Place	
Promotion	

Not-for-profit marketing

In the past, marketing was considered only applicable to the world of business, and deemed by some as inappropriate to use in the non-profit sector. However, marketing has now successfully been extended to this sector, and applied to charities, local government, schools, political parties, hospitals, churches and museums.

The main difference between not-for-profit marketing and commercial marketing is that of the objectives they are looking to meet. Businesses exist primarily to satisfy the needs of shareholders, by increasing the value of their investments in the business. Not-for-profit organisations exist to serve another group of stakeholders, such as beneficiaries of a charity, or local residents in a housing association, whose needs are often met by a service rather than in financial terms.

It is not surprising therefore, that if organisational objectives differ, then the marketing mix for such organisations will also differ.

Product

Some organisations create physical products to sell to raise funds – museums and leisure services often sell goods (mementos in the first case, and sports equipment and clothing in the latter). More often than not, the non-profit organisation is marketing a service, and so the basic service marketing characteristics apply to them, just as they do to other profit making businesses.

Price

These are "set" on a very different basis. Taking the example of leisure services provided by a local council, prices might not actually cover the cost of running the service. The lower prices might be part of a community package to benefit the local community, and might therefore be supplemented by local taxes.

Place

In recent years there have been changes in "place" decisions, particularly for charities, many of whom have taken up High Street premises to sell goods made or donated, to raise funds.

Promotion

The marketing spend tends to be limited by financial constraints, and also by the perception of stakeholders that it is wasting valuable resources that would be better spent contributing to the cause. Image is a key message for these organisations. Some national charities now use highly targeted campaigns with emotional messages to encourage donations (see the Case Study at the end of this Session).

When communicating with its "publics", any organisation needs to ensure that it is sending appropriate messages to the particular target audiences. In the case of a charity, these audiences will include existing donors, supporters, collectors, etc.

To illustrate the importance of considering all stakeholders when putting together a promotional mix for a charity, let's look at an example of how actions might be perceived.

A "guerrilla marketing stunt" could be used to create awareness, and can create quite an impact if done correctly. Such an activity might be very useful to a charity in attracting funds from new donors. However, the charity would need to forecast the results of the activity very carefully (more carefully perhaps than a commercial organisation), as regular donors would certainly take a dim view of their donations being used to fund a stunt that does not break-even. Unfortunately, unlike other forms of promotion that can be pre-tested, this type of event relies to some extent on a "surprise" element. The impact of this would be lost if a "test" was carried out.

Planners need to carefully consider the cost of the stunt, forecast the likely return, and communicate its plan to existing stakeholders.

An American charity, charitycounts.com, used a stunt that involved dropping 8,000 wallets on the streets of Manhattan just before Christmas. We can consider two options for this stunt:

1. A helicopter is hired to drop expensive leather wallets onto the pavements of Manhattan, to attract the attention of affluent shoppers and appeal to them to make donations through the web site. This would be very expensive!

2. Existing volunteers walk around Manhattan dropping plastic wallets that have been manufactured by a firm that supplies promotional gifts very cheaply as its contribution to the charity. These also contain a card appealing for donations through the web site.

The second of these options would be a more acceptable way of using charity funds.

> **Activity 11.2**
>
> Identify a non-profit organisation that you believe has been successful in adopting the marketing concept. Give specific reasons to justify your choice.

Business-to-business marketing

Differences in the marketing mix for business-to-business marketers are driven by the differences in the characteristics of the products they supply, and the buyer behaviour of the sector (covered in Session 8).

Business-to-business marketing can be categorised by the nature of the purchase. This in turn will affect the complexity of the DMU, and the length of the buying process. There are three main purchase types to be considered.

- New task purchase.
- Modified re-buy.
- Straight re-buy.

The marketing mix for each of these three types of purchase will differ, because of the nature of the purchase being made.

- New tasks tend to be major purchases, with a complex DMU involved, and a long lead-time before the purchase is made. New tasks can also be high volume, low value purchases, for example stationery, and then the situation will be less complex.
- Modified re-buys will be simpler, provided the original product or service has met expectations. Customers may want faster delivery, or a slight modification to the product. In this case personal selling will be particularly useful, as negotiations and personalisation of approach is necessary.
- Straight re-buys occur when businesses are reordering fairly straightforward products, such as consumables for use in the business, or standard components for use in manufacturing their own products.

The general differences in the marketing mix for FMCG and business-to-business markets are as follows:

Product

It is just as important for business-to-business marketers to differentiate their offering from their competitors as it is for consumer marketers. Often the products supplied are more complex than consumer products, and are much more likely to include service both before and after the sale takes place. For example, technical advice may be provided before the sale, and user training afterwards.

Price

There is often more negotiation involved in decisions about price in business-to-business markets. In addition, for some companies it is standard to have to "bid" for business by set dates. Using the Internet, some organisations are now using reverse auctions to request tenders for business. Bidders at these auctions undercut each other for the privilege of winning the tender.

Place

Distribution channels for industrial goods tend to be shorter than those for consumer goods. Many companies supply their products direct to the user company, using their own sales force to complete the business. Issues such as transport arrangements, storage of products, and inventory control, are all important to these companies.

Promotion

The promotional mix for business-to-business markets differs from consumer markets in several ways. Some businesses supply a few major customers, and so the use of personal selling is a much more feasible option for them. Products and services are often quite complex, and so the salesperson can explain face to face much more easily than a "blanket" approach in printed media. The buying unit within the customer organisation can also be complex, and the salesperson needs to develop relationships with the decision makers, adapting the message to address individual concerns. Advertising is often limited to appropriate trade journals and magazines, and usually has a more logical than emotional message.

Marketing Fundamentals

> **Activity 11.3**
>
> Your company is about to launch a new development in batteries. Your new batteries hold their charge four times longer than the average battery. Your target market includes manufacturers of laptop computers, providers of mobile phones, and retail outlets that supply peripherals for both these items.
>
> Suggest an appropriate marketing mix for the launch of this new product.

Case Study – Focusing on the future

Barnardo's campaign strengthened the brand's image both internally and externally and set the charity apart from its competitors.

By mid 1999, Barnardo's "deservedness" had eroded in relation to other charities, such as the NSPCC and Save the Children. Although Barnardo's ceased running homes for orphans over 30 years ago, this was still the connection the majority of the public made with the charity's name.

Campaign objectives

Barnardo's needed to overwrite the culturally imprinted association with homes, and replace it with modern day reality. Additionally, it had to address the problem of the confused, unfocused brand perception of its own staff. 'The challenge was to develop a new brand vision for Barnardo's that would act as a point of focus and a "rallying cry" for all their employees, and a strategic platform for all future communications to every stakeholder audience', says Penni Herriman, Account Director at the charity's advertising agency, Bartle Bogle Hegarty.

Business strategy

For the first time, the "marketing and communications" and the "social policy and research" functions within the organisation worked collaboratively to develop the vision and share it with the charity's staff. This ensured a shared belief and sense of pride in the repositioning.

Obstacles encountered

Barnardo's had limited money and channels available to sell-in and communicate the new vision and advertising to its 5,000 staff across 8 regional centres. A brand advocacy model was employed to address the challenges posed by a decentralised organisation that lacked marketing buy-in and focus. "Brand Ambassadors" from different parts of the charity went out to communicate and run consultative sessions with each internal stakeholder audience. Subsequently, the new vision and strategy featured in staff newsletters and on the organisation's Intranet.

Milestones

In October 1999, Barnardo's launched its high profile national press campaign which ran for four months, promoting the umbrella philosophy behind the charity's work: "Giving Children Back their Future". A series of four ads dramatised the preventative role of Barnardo's in children's lives, highlighting the potentially disastrous futures awaiting them without the charity's help. A telephone number and web address was included on the ads to enable people to obtain more information or make a donation. The advertisements, aimed at the core target audience of 30-54 year olds, appeared in the daily national broadsheets and weekend supplements. Quality positions and full-page executions were chosen to help build credibility and stature.

(**Update** – a new series of ads has recently been launched. You can see these on their web site www.barnardos.org.uk).

Evidence of success

The limited media budget of £1 million needed to work hard, particularly coming in the wake of a strong NSPCC campaign. Controversy over Barnardo's heroin baby ad generated £630,000 worth of media coverage (Source: Aylings).

Brand support

Work has since been carried out to ensure that all internal communications support and reflect the brand image created by the advertising campaign. New direct marketing campaigns have been launched, with the various communications agencies involved working closely together to achieve a cohesive approach.

Source: Extract from 'Focusing on the Future', *Marketing Business*, July/August 2001.

Questions

1. What was the objective Barnardo's were looking to achieve?

2. Who are its key audiences for this message?

3. List the promotional mix outlined in the Case Study and what the main issues are surrounding it, bearing in mind the fact that they are a charity.

SUMMARY OF KEY POINTS

In this Session we have explored various contexts in which the specific characteristics of the situation mean the marketing mix needs to be adapted, and have covered the following key points:

- The differences in the marketing mixes appropriate for various contexts are driven by the characteristics and objectives of the organisation, and the nature of the customer groups they are targeting.
- SMEs are often constrained by a lack of marketing budget.
- Non-profit organisations have to satisfy many publics and have very different objectives to businesses.
- Business-to-business marketing differs from consumer marketing because of the nature of the product/service and organisational buyers.
- Business-to-business marketing can also differ because of the nature of the purchase being made – new task, modified re-buy or straight re-buy.

Improving and developing own learning

The following projects are designed to help you develop your knowledge and skills further, by carrying out some research yourself. Feedback is not provided for this type of learning because there are no "answers" to be found, but you may wish to discuss your findings with colleagues and fellow students.

Marketing in differing contexts

> **Project A**
>
> Identify which sector your own organisation fits into, and how this impacts on the marketing mix employed.

> **Project B**
>
> Collect some information from a charity (perhaps use its web site as a starting point), and compare its promotional messages with those of your organisation.

> **Project C**
>
> A tea company supplies tea bags to supermarkets for sale to consumers, and also to catering businesses for use in canteens, restaurants etc. Contrast the marketing mixes they will need to adopt for each type of market.

Feedback to activities

Activity 11.1

A suggested marketing mix for a small business marketing hand-made cards and gifts might be as follows:

Product	Hand-made cards. Specialist gift items – jewellery. Packaging ready for display.
Price	Price per item. Minimum order number. Discounts for large orders and high frequency. Guidance given to retailers as to margin.
Place	Via retailers within 50 mile radius. Craft Fairs. Web site.
Promotion	Specialist magazines – PR and advertising. Local press. Personal selling.

Activity 11.2

This will depend on the organisation you select, an example is shown below.

Trade Organisation

Focused on benefits for its members.

Good internal communications.

Service standards set and met.

Mission statement demonstrates its customer focus, and this is managed and supported by top officials.

Annual research of members needs carried out.

Activity 11.3

There are no absolutely right or wrong answers here. The following shows one way it could be done.

Product	Design, packaging etc. need to be consistent with brand image.
Price	This is a new product development. Prices may initially be high to recover the development costs. Alternatively, a penetration strategy may be used, with low prices to capture market share quickly. Discounts may be negotiated for bulk purchases.
Place	Key Account Management may be appropriate for the 3 target markets*: ■ Laptop manufacturers. ■ Mobile phone manufacturers. ■ Retailers. Direct selling approach may be used.
Promotion	PR in specialist press and national business press. Advertising in specialist trade press. Personal selling.

*Mix may differ for each.

Session 12

Marketing Fundamentals

Marketing in international and virtual contexts

Introduction

This Session continues looking at marketing in different contexts by exploring marketing in an international context, and how the various characteristics of international marketing can affect the mix used. It also considers the use of e-marketing, and what this adds to traditional marketing for various marketing contexts, such as business to consumer (b2c) and business to business (b2b).

> **LEARNING OUTCOMES**
>
> At the end of this Session you will be able to:
>
> - Explain the global influences affecting the nature of marketing undertaken by organisations in an international context.
>
> - Explain e-delivery of service quality, and the existing and potential impacts of the virtual marketplace on the pattern of marketing activities in given contexts.

What do we mean by international marketing?

International marketing exists in many forms. It can involve a relatively small firm looking to extend their market by simply exporting a few products to another country, or it can be a large company, such as Coca-Cola, standardising their marketing mix and operating globally. The Internet is in some cases making it easier to do business internationally.

The choices available to companies looking to operate in international markets are as follows:

1. Use the same marketing mix worldwide – globalisation.

2. Adapt the promotional mix, but standardise the product. This allows advertising to take account of cultural and language differences, but cuts costs by offering the same product mix.

3. Adapt product, but standardise promotion. One example of this is the car market, where models of cars are adapted to meet the different laws on emission levels in different countries.
4. Adapt both product and promotion. Sometimes the product is adapted and consumers need to be informed of this fact through adapted promotion.
5. Introduce new products for different environments internationally.

Activity 12.1

Which of the above options would you choose for the following three products:

a. Cars.

b. Computers.

c. Fashion.

Important differences when marketing across borders

The marketing mix is a useful framework for considering the differences that may affect the way marketing is undertaken in international markets. Differences in the external environment (using PEST) will also need to be carefully considered in developing each element of the mix.

Product

The main difference that needs to be taken into account when marketing products abroad is that of national culture. Other issues such as climate, the local economy, and even the electricity supply, may also affect the product itself.

Price

Exchange rates will have an impact on pricing decisions, as well as what the local market is prepared to pay for a product. There are also additional costs involved in transporting products internationally.

Place

The infrastructure within other countries, and distribution systems generally, will vary from country to country.

Promotion

Cultural and language differences are the main considerations, as well as media availability and costs.

People

One issue is where you recruit your customer contact staff. If you use staff from your home market they may have problems with the culture and/or language. If you recruit from the local market it may be more difficult to motivate and manage them.

Process

The processes that are standard for you in your home market may not be appropriate internationally. Marketing research needs to be undertaken to check.

Physical Evidence

Again, what is acceptable and expected in the home market may not be what customers expect in an international market.

Activity 12.2

Suggest how the marketing mix might differ when marketing wine internationally.

The e-marketing mix

The marketing mix in the virtual marketplace highlights some key issues, particularly for traditional firms looking to integrate e-marketing with their existing approach.

Product

Can your product be offered online? If not, can it be "augmented" by the provision of additional benefits online? Is it possible to develop new products that can be offered online?

Price

One of the characteristics of online consumers is that they tend to be cash rich and time poor. This means that they are perhaps more interested in convenience than making savings, although the Internet is enabling greater price transparency (and so easier comparison of prices across competitors). In business-to-business (b2b) markets new pricing models are emerging. Reverse auctions are one example of this, and these were covered in the last Session.

Place

Some products can be supplied from the web; music and software for example can be purchased and downloaded immediately. Information can also be provided in the form of electronic documents, and e-books are gradually becoming more popular. However, these are the exceptions, and although products can be purchased online, most still need a traditional delivery or transportation service. In Session 7, we dealt with disintermediation, and the fact that wholesalers actually provide very valuable services at their point in the channel. It is important to remember that cutting out the middleman does not always result in cost savings.

Promotion

This has been covered in Session 8. However, it is useful to link traditional promotional techniques to their online equivalents, and this is done below.

Traditional	Online
Advertising.	Banner ads.
Personal selling.	Affiliate marketing.
Sales promotion.	Online coupons, loyalty points, etc.
PR.	Portals, features, corporate web sites, e-newsletters.
Sponsorship.	Sponsorship of another site or online event.
Direct mail.	Email (preferably opt-in).
Exhibitions.	Some exhibitions are now put online.
Word-of-mouth.	Viral marketing.

People

Call-back facilities, where staff in a call centre call-back the web user at their request, are becoming more and more common, with the aim of providing personal contact for those people that want it. FAQ pages and contact by email also provide substitutes for personal contact.

Process

This is an important part of e-marketing. Many processes can be enhanced through electronic means. However, many companies' processes are often not enhanced because of simple omissions or the fact that they are not thoroughly thought through. Are there processes in place to respond quickly to customer emails? Are there systems available for customers to check the progress of their order? Is there a system to notify customers if the product they order online is not in stock?

Physical evidence

When marketing online, physical evidence is there to reassure the potential customer, just as it does off-line through the provision of an "image" the customer can associate with. People are still cautious about buying online, and messages about the way in which refunds are dealt with, and how information is kept private, can help reassure customers.

Whatever decisions are made about online activity, it is important to remember that it must be co-ordinated with your off-line mix. Whether an organisation is looking to supplement and update their activity through the use of e-marketing, or looking to offer a virtual presence only, there will be a need to use both online and off-line marketing tools, and these must offer a consistent message to customers and potential customers.

Activity 12.3

Visit www.amazon.com. Look at the information provided by them about the services they offer. Try to find evidence of each element of the e-marketing mix and make notes about your findings.

Case Study – Central reservations

Below-the-line marketing* has only recently become prevalent in Central Europe. Mark Zimmer of Mosaic Group Marketing Services looks at how things are changing, and changing fast.

It's hard to believe that it's ten years since the Berlin Wall came down, but among all the pre-millennium celebrations last December, this was one event which still attracted a good deal of media attention.

Much has changed in Central Europe in the decade since that event; indeed some places are almost unrecognisable. Western brands have made massive and swift in-roads onto the high streets – you'll find branches of Tesco in Hungary for example. This was probably to be expected, but what has perhaps been unexpected is the relatively slow advance of what we know as "below-the-line" marketing*. As the major multinationals have moved in, the advertising agencies have moved in with them. No surprises there. But with a few exceptions, the specialist agencies with which we are now so familiar just haven't made any impression.

This is surprising indeed. After all, this is a market of 130 to 150 million people. Disposable income is rising. The economies of the region are maturing rapidly. In areas like financial services things are set to boom as the new millennium advances. For some states like Poland, Hungary and the Czech Republic, EU membership can only be a few years away. But where are the specialists in sales promotion? Where are the field marketers? Where are the marketing events companies?

It's not that these things don't happen – in some areas they are done very well. But the majority of promotional campaigns are a mixed bag, and the overall quality has a rather dated feel to it, looking like campaigns in the UK did 15 years ago. This is partly because the advertising agencies have given below-the-line promotions away. They have been bolted on to the main advertising as a poorly executed afterthought. They've used such campaigns to add value to their existing service offering, but done little to provide good service or add real creative and strategic input. That is, up until now.

Mosaic Group Marketing Services has had an office in Turkey for over a year. In December we opened an office in Vienna (under the agency name ZGC Vienna), and as the New Year progresses we will be making further announcements in Hungary and Poland. Clearly we will go where our clients want us to go, but I am also convinced that the mood is changing and the demand now is for the specialist consultancy to take centre stage. Companies and brands in Central Europe want more from promotional marketing and events. They recognise that these are playing an increasing part in the marketing mix, and they want to get more from both their agencies and the promotions they are developing. Provided they can show real value, the specialists can win new business, and below-the-line marketing will be the major growth area in this market.

I don't expect Mosaic Group will be the only agency to have spotted this trend and be ready to exploit it. Indeed, I'd be happy to welcome others into the marketplace, as it should help to expand the market overall. But by adopting a regional approach, with five or six strategically-sited offices, I believe we will be better placed than any others to take full advantage of this trend, and will grow that new business faster. It's a long time now since the wall physically came down. Though here in the "West" I expect we're all getting a bit tired of talking about "integration" and its benefits, in Central Europe the benefits of specialism are just coming into focus. It would be ironic to start putting up new walls between the different types of agencies. The clients want better work, and they are now anxious to find the dedicated agencies to provide just that.

Source: 'Central Reservations', *Marketing Business*, March 2000.

*Below-the-line – non-media advertising or promotion for which no commission has been paid to the advertising agency.

Questions

1. The Case Study highlights some of the different approaches to promotion that exist in Central Europe. What reasons are given for this in the Case?

2. Why might it be better to use a local agency when arranging promotional activity in an international market?

SUMMARY OF KEY POINTS

In this Session we have explored the international and virtual contexts for marketing, and covered the following key points:

- There are several options for entering international markets, involving different degrees of adaptation and standardisation.

- The marketing mix used in international markets is influenced by PEST factors, and also by local culture.

- E-marketing has an equivalent marketing mix, and online and off-line activity needs to be integrated.

Improving and developing own learning

The following projects are designed to help you develop your knowledge and skills further, by carrying out some research yourself. Feedback is not provided for this type of learning because there are no "answers" to be found, but you may wish to discuss your findings with colleagues and fellow students.

Project A

Find out whether your organisation markets internationally. What degree of standardisation/adaptation exists?

Project B

Talk to someone in your Marketing Department about the marketing mix used in any international market. What differences can you identify for each of the 7 Ps?

Project C

Look at your own company's web site, or one you are familiar with, and make notes about the effectiveness of the physical evidence element of the e-marketing mix.

Special project – Marketing and the law

It is very important that marketers today are aware of the areas of legislation and regulation that impact upon them in their day-to-day role. You do not need to be an expert – your organisation will either employ a corporate lawyer, or use an external firm.

Find out how the following affect the way your organisation carries out its marketing:

- The Advertising Standards Agency (ASA).
- Consumer Protection.

- Data Protection.
- Contract Law.
- Trading Standards.
- Misrepresentation.
- Competition Law.
- Copyright.
- Trade Marks.

Feedback to activities

Activity 12.1

The answers to this activity will depend on a large number of factors. However, the following are reasonable options:

a. Cars – adapted mix for product and promotion (legal, language).

b. Computers – globalisation.

c. Fashion – new products developed for each market.

Activity 12.2

Wine will not be appropriate for some international markets, as some religions forbid alcohol. Elsewhere the following may be the major issues:

Product – standard, although labelling may be adapted.

Price – may be affected by local taxation, otherwise standardised.

Place – decisions about licensing bottling to local markets to ease transportation. If not, decisions about air or sea transportation.

Promotion – Internet, and then within the constraints of local markets. Language would have to be accommodated.

Activity 12.3

Amazon.com are now well established and have learned initial lessons from dealing online.

Product – they have extended their product range to include other items that sell well online. These include books, music, video, electronics and software.

Price – discounts offered on book prices. Options offered for delivery charges.

Place – Internet only.

Promotion – PR, portals, other sites, associate programme (commission is offered to associates who have a link to amazon from their own site).

People – very little contact. However, on the one occasion we have had to contact, the response was efficient and pleasant.

Process – excellent order system, good refund policy, can track orders online, orders followed up by email to confirm status – i.e. order confirmed, order despatched.

Physical evidence – easy to navigate site, opportunity to interact.

Glossary

Glossary

The following relevant terms have been taken from the CIM's online glossary. If you would like to see a full listing of marketing terms please visit www.cim.co.uk, and look under Services and then the Library and Information Service section of the site.

Above-the-line – advertising for which a payment is made and for which a commission is paid to the advertising agency.

Account management – the process by which an agency or supplier manages the needs of a client.

ACORN – a classification of residential neighbourhoods. It is a database that divides up the entire population of the UK in terms of the housing in which they live.

Added value – the increase in worth of a product or service as a result of a particular activity. In the context of marketing this might be packaging or branding.

Advertising – promotion of a product, service or message by an identified sponsor using paid-for media.

AIDA (Attention, Interest, Desire, Action) – a model describing the process that advertising or promotion is intended to initiate in the mind of a prospective customer.

Ansoff matrix – model relating marketing strategy to general strategic direction. It maps product/market strategies.

BCG (Boston Consulting Group) Matrix – model for product portfolio analysis.

Below-the-line – non-media advertising or promotion when no commission has been paid to the advertising agency.

Brand – the set of physical attributes of a product or service, together with the beliefs and expectations surrounding it.

Business plan – a strategic document showing cash flow, forecasts and direction of a company.

Business strategy – the means by which a business works towards achieving its stated aims.

Business to business (b2b) – relating to the sale of a product or service for any use other than personal consumption.

Business to consumer (b2c) – relating to the sale of a product or service for personal consumption.

Buying behaviour – the process that buyers go through when deciding whether or not to purchase goods or services.

Channels – the methods used by a company to communicate and interact with its customers.

Competitive advantage – the product, proposition or benefit that puts a company ahead of its competitors.

Consumer – individual who buys and uses a product or service.

Consumer behaviour – the buying habits and patterns of consumers in the acquisition and usage of products and services.

Copyright – the law that protects the originator's material from unauthorised use, usually (in the UK) for seventy years after the originator's death.

Corporate identity – the character a company seeks to establish for itself in the mind of the public.

Corporate reputation – a complex mix of characteristics such as ethos, identity and image that go to make up a company's public personality.

Culture – a shared set of values, beliefs and traditions that influence prevailing behaviour within a country or organisation.

Customer – a person or company who purchases goods or services.

Customer loyalty – feelings or attitudes that incline a customer to return to a company, shop or outlet to purchase there again.

Customer Relationship Management (CRM) – the coherent management of contacts and interactions with customers.

Customer satisfaction – the provision of goods or services that fulfil the customer's expectations in terms of quality and service, in relation to the price paid.

Data processing – the obtaining, recording and holding of information which can then be retrieved, used, disseminated or erased.

Data Protection Act – a UK law which makes organisations responsible for protecting the privacy of personal data.

Database marketing – whereby customer information stored in an electronic database is utilised for targeting marketing activities.

Decision-Making Unit (DMU) – the team of people in an organisation or family group who make the final buying decision.

Demographic data – information describing and segmenting a population in terms of age, sex, income and so on, which can be used to target marketing campaigns.

Differentiation – ensuring that products and services have a unique element to allow them to stand out from the rest.

Direct mail – delivery of an advertising or promotional message to customers or potential customers by mail.

Direct marketing – all activities that make it possible to offer goods or services or to transmit other messages to a segment of the population by post, telephone, email or other direct means.

Distribution (Place) – the process of getting the goods from the manufacturer or supplier to the user.

Diversification – an increase in the variety of goods and services produced by an organisation.

E-commerce – business conducted electronically.

E-marketing – marketing conducted electronically.

Electronic Point of Sale (EPOS) – a system whereby electronic tills are used to process customer transactions in a retail outlet.

Ethical marketing – marketing that takes account of the moral aspects of decisions.

Export marketing – the marketing of goods or services to overseas customers.

Field marketing – extending an organisation's marketing in the field through merchandising, product launches, training of retail staff, etc.

FMCG (Fast Moving Consumer Goods) – such as food and toiletries.

Focus groups – a tool for marketing research where small groups of participants take part in guided discussions on the topic being researched.

Forecasting – calculation of future events and performance.

Franchising – the selling of a licence by the owner (franchiser) to a third party (franchisee) permitting the sale of a product or service for a specified period.

Geodemographics – a method of analysis combining geographic and demographic variables.

Grey market (silver market) – term used to define a population over a certain age (usually 65).

Industrial marketing (or business-to-business marketing) – the marketing of industrial products.

Innovation – development of new products, services or ways of working.

Internal customers – employees within an organisation can be viewed as "consumers" of products or services provided by another part of the organisation.

Internal marketing – the process of eliciting support for a company and its activities among its own employees in order to encourage them to promote its goals.

International marketing – the conduct and co-ordination of marketing activities in more than one country.

Key Account Management (KAM) – account management as applied to a company's most valuable customers.

Logo – a graphic usually consisting of a symbol and or group of letters that identifies a company or brand.

Macro-environment – the external factors which affect companies' planning and performance, and that are beyond its control (PEST or SLEPT factors).

Market development – the process of growing sales by offering existing products (or new versions of them) to new customer groups.

Market penetration – the attempt to grow business by obtaining a larger market share in an existing market.

Market research – the gathering and analysis of data relating to markets to inform decision making.

Marketing research – the gathering and analysis of data relating to marketing to inform decision making (includes product research, place research, pricing research, etc).

Market segmentation – the division of the marketplace into distinct sub-groups or segments, each characterised by particular tastes and requiring a specific marketing mix.

Market share – a company's sales of a given product or set of products to a given set of customers, expressed as a percentage of total sales of all such products to such customers.

Marketing audit – scrutiny of an organisation's existing marketing system to ascertain its strengths and weaknesses.

Marketing communications (Promotion) – all methods used by a firm to communicate with its customers and stakeholders.

Marketing information – any information used or required to support marketing decisions.

Marketing mix – the combination of marketing inputs that affect customer motivation and behaviour (7 Ps – Product, Price, Promotion, Place, People, Process and Physical evidence).

Marketing orientation – a business strategy whereby customers' needs and wants determine corporate direction.

Marketing planning – the selection and scheduling of activities to support the company's chosen marketing strategy or goals.

Marketing strategy – the broad methods chosen to achieve marketing objectives.

Micro-environment – the immediate context of a company's operations, including such elements as suppliers, customers and competitors.

Mission statement – a company's summary of its business philosophy, purpose and direction.

Model – simplified representation of a process, designed to aid understanding.

New Product Development (NPD) – the creation of new products, from evaluation of proposals through to launch.

Niche marketing – the marketing of a product to a small and well-defined segment of the marketplace.

Objectives – a company's defined and measurable aims or goals for a given period.

Packaging – material used to protect and promote goods.

Personal selling – one-to-one communication between the seller and a prospective purchaser.

PEST – a framework for viewing the macro-environment; Political, Economic, Social and Technical factors.

Positioning – the creation of an image for a product or service in the minds of customers, both specifically to that item and in relation to competitive offerings.

Product Life Cycle (PLC) – a model describing the progress of a product from the inception of the idea, through its growth and maturity to its eventual decline.

Promotional mix – the components of an individual campaign, which is likely to include advertising, personal selling, public relations, direct marketing, packaging and sales promotion.

Public Relations (PR) – planned and sustained communications to promote a mutual understanding between an organisation and its stakeholders.

Qualitative research – information that cannot be measured or expressed in numeric terms. It is useful to the marketer as it often explores people's feelings and opinions.

Quantitative research – information that can be measured in numeric terms and analysed statistically.

Reference group – a group with which the customer identifies in some way and whose opinions and experiences influence the customer's behaviour.

Glossary

Relationship marketing – the strategy of establishing relationships with customers which continues well beyond their first purchases.

Sales promotion – a range of techniques used to increase sales in the short term.

Skimming – the pricing policy of setting the original price high in the early stages of the product life cycle to get as much profit as possible before prices are driven down by increasing competition.

SLEPT – a framework for viewing the macro-environment; Socio-cultural, Legal, Economic, Political and Technical factors.

SMART – a mnemonic referring to the need for objectives to be Specific, Measurable, Achievable, Relevant and Time-bound.

Sponsorship – specialised form of promotion where a company will help fund an event or support a business venture in return for publicity.

Stakeholder – an individual or group that affects or is affected by the organisation and its operations.

Supplier – an organisation or individual that supplies goods or services to a company.

Targeting – the use of market segmentation to select and address a key group of potential purchasers.

Unique Selling Proposition (USP) – the benefit that a product or service can deliver to customers that is not offered by any competitors.

Vision – the long-term aims and aspirations of the company for itself.

Word-of-mouth – the spreading of information through human interaction alone.

Appendix 1

Appendix 1

Feedback to Case Studies

Session 1

1. **What categories of "customer value" are identified in the Case Study?**

    Lower prices implied – through use of reverse auctions to drive down costs.
    Information – about its products and on parenting.
    Association – customers involved in pre-launch research.
    Convenience – response to customer queries.

2. **How is Procter & Gamble achieving improved "value for money"?**

    By using reverse auctions to drive down the costs of raw materials. These reductions in cost can then be passed onto customers as reductions in prices.

3. **Procter & Gamble are building relationships through email contact. Suggest three ways they can ensure this effort does not fail.**

    Ask permission to contact.
    Ensure a fast response to queries.
    Offer an e-newsletter as a regular form of contact.

Session 2

1. **How is the organisation described before it had a marketing plan in place?**

    Ad hoc.
    Not very impressive.

2. **What specific actions can you identify that were taken as a result of the plan being in place?**

    New corporate identity developed.
    New logo and house style.
    Press campaign (advertising and editorial).
    Quarterly newsletter.
    Clean database.
    Professional sales packs.

3. **What results of the plan can you identify?**

   Core values retained.
   Ten-fold increase in editorial coverage.

Session 3

1. **What are the three segments identified in the Case Study?**

   "Thrivers" – most affluent, active and healthy.
   "Seniors" – concerned with health issues and personal comfort.
   "Elders" – free of debt and intend to stay that way.

2. **Which segment might be best to target for a new design of open top, high-performance car?**

   Thrivers – those in their 50s.

3. **Identify three examples of approaches to communication that the Case Study highlights as being relevant to these segments.**

   Use familiar language in communication.
   Direct mail appropriate – they warm to personal communication.
   High level of customer care.

Session 4

1. **Describe the "people" element of the marketing mix that needs to exist for Interflora.**

   Positive team of customer-facing or phone contact staff.
   Good product knowledge.
   Friendly and approachable image.
   Professional approach.
   Efficient processing – minimum human error.

2. **Describe the "process" element of the marketing mix that needs to exist for Interflora.**

   Seamless process from the customers' perspective.
   Setting of service standards.
   Sufficient resources to implement processes.
   Internet order tracking.
   24-hour helpline.

Appendix 1

3. **Describe the "physical evidence" element of the marketing mix that needs to exist for Interflora.**

   Décor appropriate for customer service.
   Brand on uniforms.
   Brand featured on premises and literature.

Session 5

1. **What developments were made to the product in 1999, 10 years after its launch?**

   New flavour.
   New packaging.

2. **What was the major risk that Müller were taking in terms of the launch in 1989?**

   New pot size – their product was targeted at the "healthy eating" sector, so a large part of their target audience was made up of dieters. A larger pot might not be attractive to them.

3. **What did the newly developed product achieve through its relaunch?**

   The % of target audience acknowledging the product as their favourite increased by 9%.

   57% "end-line" recall within 15 months of the start of the campaign.

   Growth in market share to 12.8% in a declining market.

Session 6

1. **Identify the types of information that will be useful in setting the price for a new pair of football boots.**

   Relative strength of the brand against competitors.
   Trends in footwear market and football.
   Corporate objectives.
   Costs of development of the new product and general production costs.
   Likely demand for product.
   Research into what price the market will stand.

2. **Suggest the most appropriate pricing method for the new football boots.**

   Demand-based pricing (also known as market-based pricing).

Session 7

1. **What advantages and disadvantages might car manufacturers gain through using supermarkets as part of their channel to market?**

   Advantages – high volume sales.

   Disadvantages – buyer power used to reduce prices, forcing manufacturers to cut costs.

2. **What advantages and disadvantages might car manufacturers gain through using Internet dealers as part of their channel to market?**

   Advantages – high volume sales.

   Disadvantages – widely dispersed market, possible increased transport costs.

3. **What advantages and disadvantages might car manufacturers gain through staying with the traditional channel of dealerships?**

   Advantages – dealing with "known" member of the channel, can control prices better.

   Disadvantages – limited choice available for consumers.

Session 8

1. **What was the challenge faced by Skoda's new Marketing Manager?**

   Deep-rooted brand prejudice against the product.

   Lack of past action – proper research conducted, but there had been no adequate response.

   Current advertising was not working.

2. **What was the message communicated by the new campaign?**

   "It's a Skoda. Honest." was used to get people to re-evaluate the product.

Appendix 1

3. **List the full range of promotional tools used in the new campaign.**

   TV advertising, poster campaign, press advertising, personal selling (training of sales staff), product placement and integrated PR (editorial in press, TV and radio).

Session 9

1. **Explain how the "people" element of the marketing mix can be used effectively for legal firms.**

   Knowledgeable, helpful staff – customer contact.
   Qualifications of the professional staff.
   Junior staff networking effectively.

2. **What promotional activity can you identify from the Case Study?**

   Networking and increased contact with clients.
   Brand building through advertising.
   Communication via the web site.
   Developing practices to encourage client loyalty.
   Corporate hospitality.
   Telemarketing (accountancy firms).

3. **How might marketing audits help the legal firms that have started to market their practices?**

   Help analyse company performance.
   Identify most profitable clients and services.
   Provide information on what services clients use.
   Help evaluate effective use of promotional tools.

Session 10

1. **Identify the three measures of marketing effectiveness that Skoda used in the Case Study.**

   Company market share.
   Overall sale of product (Fabia).
   Market share of the small car segment.

Marketing Fundamentals

2. **Explain two further measures that they could have used.**

   Media coverage of advertising and PR activity.
   Target sales by value.

3. **Explain the difference between <u>quantitative</u> and <u>qualitative</u> measures, using examples from the Case Study to illustrate your answer.**

   Quantitative measures are statistics and figures, such as cost analysis. An example from the Case Study is the number of Skodas sold between January-May 1999, compared to January-May 2000.

   Qualitative measures identify awareness, perception, satisfaction, etc. An example from the Case Study is the improvement in people's perception that Skodas were better than they used to be, and people imagining themselves driving Skodas.

   Often a mixture of both methods is used.

Session 11

1. **What was the objective Barnardo's were looking to achieve?**

   Re-establish the brand and give it a clear identity.

2. **Who are its key audiences for this message?**

   Organisation stakeholders – in particular, employees and potential donors (core audience of 30-54 year olds).

3. **List the promotional mix that was outlined in the Case Study and what the main issues are surrounding it, bearing in mind the fact that they are a charity.**

   Press advertising, internal brand awareness communication, web site, direct marketing.

   Constraints included limited budget and channels. The campaign needed to be high profile, but not seen to be glossy or trivial.

Appendix 1

Session 12

1. **The Case Study highlights some of the different approaches to promotion that exist in Central Europe. What reasons are given for this in the Case?**

   The Case Study identifies that advertising agencies are currently "giving away" below-the-line promotions.

2. **Why might it be better to use a local agency when arranging promotional activity in an international market?**

   A local agency will have a better understanding of the local culture, and a greater knowledge of the language, competitors and market structure.

Appendix 2

Appendix 2

Syllabus

Marketing fundamentals

Aim

The Marketing Fundamentals module develops a basic knowledge and understanding of marketing, marketing process and the marketing mix. It aims to provide participants with a framework on which to build marketing knowledge and skills through the modules of this Certificate Stage, through modules at later Stages, and in the workplace.

Participants will not be expected to have any prior knowledge or experience in a marketing role.

Related statements of practice

Bb.2   Contribute to the production of marketing plans and budgets.

Db.1   Contribute to the development of products and services.

Eb.1   Contribute to the development of pricing policies.

Eb.2   Implement pricing policies.

Fb.1   Develop effective channels to market.

Fb.2   Provide support to channel members.

Hb.1   Contribute to planning and budget preparation.

Learning outcomes

Participants will be able to:

- Explain the development of marketing and the ways it can benefit business and organisations.
- Identify the main steps in, and barriers to, achieving a marketing orientation within the organisation.
- Explain the context of, and process for, marketing planning and budgeting, including related models.

- Explain the concept of segmentation and the different bases for effective market segmentation.
- Identify and describe the individual elements and tools of the marketing mix.
- Identify the basic differences in application of the marketing mix involved in marketing products and services within different marketing contexts.

Knowledge and skill requirements

Element 1: The development of marketing and market orientation (10%)

1.1 Explain the development of marketing as an exchange process, a philosophy of business, and a managerial function.

1.2 Recognise the contribution of marketing as a means of creating customer value and as a form of competition.

1.3 Appreciate the importance of a market orientation to organisational performance, and identify the factors that promote and impede the adoption of a market orientation.

1.4 Explain the role of marketing in co-ordinating organisational resources both within and outside the marketing function.

1.5 Describe the impact of marketing actions on society and the need for marketers to act in an ethical and socially responsible manner.

1.6 Examine the significance of buyer-seller relationships in marketing and comprehend the role of relationship marketing in facilitating the retention of customers.

Element 2: Marketing planning and budgeting (20%)

2.1 Explain the importance of the marketing planning process and where it fits into the corporate or organisational planning framework.

2.2 Explain the models that describe the various stages of the marketing planning process.

2.3 Explain the concept of the marketing audit as an appraisal of the external marketing environment and an organisation's internal marketing operations.

2.4 Describe the role of various analytical tools in the marketing auditing process.

2.5   Explain the value of marketing research and information in developing marketing plans.

2.6   Explain the importance of objectives and the influences on, and processes for, setting objectives.

2.7   Explain the concept of market segmentation and distinguish effective bases for segmenting consumer and business-to-business markets.

2.8   Describe the structure of an outline marketing plan and identify its various components.

2.9   Depict the various management structures available for implementing marketing plans, and understand their advantages and disadvantages.

2.10 Examine the factors that affect the setting of marketing budgets.

2.11 Demonstrate an appreciation of the need to monitor and control marketing activities.

Element 3: The marketing mix and related tools (50%)

3.1   Describe the essential elements of targeting and positioning, and the creation of an integrated and coherent marketing mix.

3.2   Describe the wide range of tools and techniques available to marketers to satisfy customer requirements and compete effectively.

3.3   Explain the development of the extended marketing mix concept to include additional components in appropriate contextual settings: product, price, place (distribution), promotion (communications), people, processes, physical evidence and customer service.

3.4   Demonstrate an awareness of products as bundles of benefits that deliver customer value and have different characteristics, features and levels.

3.5   Explain and illustrate the product life cycle concept and recognise its effects on marketing mix decisions.

3.6   Explain and illustrate the principles of product policy: branding, product lines, packaging and service support.

3.7   Explain the importance of introducing new products, and describe the processes involved in their development and launch.

3.8 Explore the range of internal and external factors that influence pricing decisions.

3.9 Identify and illustrate a range of different pricing policies and tactics that are adopted by organisations as effective means of competition.

3.10 Define channels of distribution, intermediaries and logistics, and understand the contribution they make to the marketing effort.

3.11 State and explain the factors that influence channel decisions and the selection of alternative distribution channel options, including the effects of new information and communications technology.

3.12 Describe the extensive range of tools that comprise the marketing communications mix, and examine the factors that contribute to its development and implementation.

3.13 Explain the importance of people in marketing and in particular the contribution of staff to effective service delivery.

3.14 Explain the importance of service in satisfying customer requirements and identify the factors that contribute to the delivery of service quality.

3.15 Examine the effects of information and communication technology on the development and implementation of the marketing mix.

3.16 Explain the importance of measuring the effectiveness of the selected marketing effort and instituting appropriate changes where necessary.

Element 4: Marketing in context (20%)

4.1 Explain the importance of contextual setting in influencing the selection of, and emphasis given to, marketing mix tools.

4.2 Explain differences in the characteristics of various types of marketing context: FMCG, business to business (supply chain), large or capital project-based, services, voluntary and not-for-profit, sales support (e.g. SMEs), and their impact on marketing mix decisions.

4.3 Compare and contrast the marketing activities of organisations that operate and compete in different contextual settings.

Appendix 2

4.4 Explain the global dimension in affecting the nature of marketing undertaken by organisations in an international environmental context.

4.5 Explain the existing and potential impact of the virtual marketplace on the pattern of marketing activities in given contexts.

Appendix 3

Appendix 3

Specimen examination paper

 The Chartered Institute of Marketing

Certificate in Marketing

Marketing Fundamentals

5.24: Marketing Fundamentals

Time:

Date:

3 Hours Duration

This examination is in two sections.

PART A – Is compulsory and worth 40% of total marks.

PART B – Has **SIX** questions; select **THREE**. Each answer will be worth 20% of the total marks.

DO NOT repeat the question in your answer, but show clearly the number of the question attempted on the appropriate pages of the answer book.

Rough workings should be included in the answer book and ruled through after use.

© The Chartered Institute of Marketing

Certificate in Marketing

5.24: Marketing Fundamentals – Specimen Paper

PART A

Energy Power Systems Launches a New Battery Range

Energy Power Systems is a division of the Ecco Battery Company (EBC) and manufactures **rechargeable** batteries. Ecco is the world's largest producer of battery and flashlight products, with twenty production facilities supplying over 500 products into 165 countries worldwide. The key corporate objectives are to increase profitability by 5% within the next two years, and for the battery division to be positioned as the number one supplier of state-of-the-art technology in batteries.

Energy Power Systems (EPS) manufactures rechargeable nickel cadmium, nickel metal hydride and lithium ion cells and battery packs for equipment manufacturers, and for the consumer market. The cells are produced at the company's headquarters in Florida, and then either sold directly to the equipment manufacturers or assembled into battery packs by one of three assembly facilities in Mexico, Newcastle (UK), or Hong Kong.

Energy Power Systems' Rechargeable Battery Product Range

EPS produces a particular range of rechargeable batteries, most of which are used in either cordless power tools, emergency lighting or mobile communications. However, the relatively inexpensive technology employed in current manufacture is being replaced by a new technology. A European directive has been issued to ban all of this type of battery by the year 2008, due to the negative impact that the cadmium electrode within the cell has on the environment when consumers dispose of these cells.

Core Markets

Energy Power Systems employs a differentiated segmentation strategy, modifying the marketing mix for each of its targeted segments. This allows the company to concentrate on markets that offer high returns and opportunities for growth, which is consistent with the corporate objectives of its parent company EBC.

Appendix 3

EPS segments the market into an industrial segment and a consumer segment, and further segments these as follows:

Industrial Segment

- Mobile communications manufacturers such as Ericsson, Motorola, etc.
- Cordless power tool manufacturers.
- Computer manufacturers.

Consumer Segments

- Audio visual equipment – e.g. Sony Walkman.
- Personal care – such as the cordless toothbrush.
- Photographic – e.g. camera batteries.
- Toys and novelties.
- Hand-held equipment – such as cordless car vacuum cleaners.

New Product Range – 'Smart' Batteries

The company is about to launch a new range of 'smart' batteries, using a relatively new type of technology. These batteries have the ability to control their own charging when fitted into a compatible charger. They also have the ability to report back information to the user of the battery – information such as the time left till empty, manufacturer's name, age, etc.

EPS is one of the only battery manufacturers that offer in-house design and manufacture of these smart batteries. For the core industrial markets, a completely 'customer-smart' battery can go from concept to production in as little as five months.

The brand name 'Energy' is the name used for all batteries produced by the company. Recently commissioned marketing research has shown that within the consumer segments, the brand is known worldwide. However, this is less important to industrial users, who usually prefer to display their own logo on the batteries. This research has also highlighted the fact that consumers are mainly interested in the length of the battery life and reliability. The company is aiming to secure the market by being the first entrant with this 'smart' technology.

PART A

Question 1.

The launch of these new batteries is due to take place within the next year. You are to prepare a report to be used as the basis for discussion within the organisation's Marketing Department which considers:

a. The principle of market segmentation and the advantages that it offers the company.

(10 marks)

b. The various stages involved in the new product development process for the new batteries.

(15 marks)

c. The composition of the different marketing mix programmes that are adopted for the launch of the batteries into the consumer and business-to-business segments to be targeted.

(15 marks)
(40 marks in total)

Appendix 3

PART B – Answer THREE Questions Only

Question 2.

You work for a children's clothing manufacturer that intends to grow its business through new channels of distribution.

a. Identify the range of alternative distribution channels that may be available to your company.

(7 marks)

b. Identify the factors that should be taken into account when deciding which distribution channels to select.

(7 marks)

c. Identify how the effectiveness of your distribution channels may be measured.

(6 marks)
(20 marks in total)

Question 3.

a. For a service organisation of your choice, illustrate how the extended marketing mix for services is used to effectively meet customer requirements.

(12 marks)

b. Examine the part played by new information and communications technology in providing additional value for the customers of your chosen organisation.

(8 marks)
(20 marks in total)

Question 4.

You are employed by a global car manufacturer that is regarded as being a leading exponent of contemporary marketing practice. Using illustrative examples from your industry:

a. Explain what you understand to be the advantages of marketing to both consumers and business organisations.

(12 marks)

b. Identify some of the ethical and social responsibility issues that face modern marketers.

(8 marks)
(20 marks in total)

Question 5.

Your organisation, which manufactures TV and hi-fi equipment, is in the process of developing a marketing plan.

a. Describe and illustrate the structure of its outline marketing plan.

(10 marks)

b. Examine the factors that it should consider when setting its marketing budgets.

(10 marks)
(20 marks in total)

Question 6.

You have recently taken up a position as a Marketing Manager in a small computing software house that has little understanding of some of the fundamental principles of marketing. You have been asked to explain and illustrate the following in the context of this organisation:

a. Variations in the marketing mix at the different stages of the product life cycle.

(10 marks)

b. The range of internal and external factors that influence pricing decisions.

(10 marks)
(20 marks in total)

Question 7.

For a large financial services company of your choice (such as a bank):

a. Explain the concept and importance of branding.

(10 marks)

b. Explain the significance of relationship marketing and customer retention.

(10 marks)
(20 marks in total)

Appendix 4

Feedback to the specimen examination paper

The following do not represent full specimen answers to the specimen examination paper, but instead look at:

- The rationale for the question – what the examiner is looking for.
- The best way to structure your answer.
- The key points that you should have included and expanded upon.
- How marks for the question might have been allocated.
- The main syllabus area that is being assessed.

Please note that many of the key points are represented here in the form of bullet point lists. All of these points should be expanded on in your answer, unless the examiner **specifically** asks you for a bullet point list.

The timings given for each part of each question allow a little time for reading the Case Study, planning your answers, and choosing which questions you will answer. Remember to follow the instructions on the paper.

Part A

Question 1.

The Case Study for this paper is about a **manufacturer** of rechargeable batteries in the USA. It introduces the fact that the company already uses **segmentation** to target its markets, and also the fact that it is about to launch a new range of products. We can see that some key marketing issues are highlighted.

- The company already markets its products to a **global market**.
- It already uses **segmentation** to **target** selected markets.
- It is an **innovative** company, trying to stay ahead of the competition through the development of new products.
- Its products can be targeted at both **consumer** and **business-to-business** customers.

The important thing to remember about approaching the mini-case question is that you must apply the **concepts** that the examiner is looking for to the **context** and situation described in the Case. With every question that is broken up into sections, you also need to consider how the marks are spread across the various parts of the question, as this should dictate how much time you allocate to each part.

a. The examiner in this case has asked you for a **report** to be used as the basis for discussion within the organisation's marketing department. This not only tells you the format in which to answer, but the **audience** you are addressing.

   The examiner is looking for you to define **segmentation**.

   What is it?

   How does it work and what **advantages** does it offer **EPS**, especially in terms of how it helps the marketing department define a **marketing mix**?

   What are the main **bases** you can use to **segment** markets in both consumer and business-to-business markets?

   How does it relate to **targeting and positioning**?

   What does this mean for **EPS**?

   There are 10 marks for this part of the question, so you should spend approximately 15 minutes answering it.

   Syllabus reference – 2.7 and 3.1.

b. This part of the question focuses on the development of the new range of batteries.

   First you should identify why the **NPD process** is important. It is then looking for you to identify each stage of the new product development process and link it to the material in the case.

   Idea generation.
   Screening of new ideas.
   Business analysis.
   Product development.
   Test marketing.
   Launch.

There are 15 marks for this part of the question, so you should spend roughly 22-23 minutes answering it.

Syllabus reference – 3.7.

c. The final part of this compulsory question looks for you to outline the two **contrasting marketing mixes** that would be used for the launch of the batteries to both the **consumer** and the **business-to-business** markets.

You may want to introduce this section with a brief explanation of the reasons why the mixes will differ – **differing buyer behaviour and market characteristics**.

One way of presenting the remainder of your answer would be in a table (see below), showing the main differences in each area of the mix. You would then conclude with a summary.

	Consumer	Business to Business
Product		
Price		
Promotion		
Place		

There are 15 marks for this part of the question, so again you should spend roughly 22-23 minutes answering it.

Syllabus reference – 4.1 and 4.2.

Appendix 4

Part B (You are asked to choose 3 from 6 questions in this section)

Question 2.

a. First of all, note that there is no format given in which to answer this question. Although this is the case, you should ensure that you structure your answer in a **logical** way, and make it **businesslike** in approach. Use sub-headings to **signpost** the examiner through your answer, and leave a space between each sub-section, so the examiner is not faced with a "wall of words".

Note that the context of the question is that of a **children's clothing manufacturer**, and keep this in mind as you start to describe the range of **distribution channels** available.

Key points will include:

What does a distribution channel do?
Outline available options and those suitable for the context:

Perhaps direct; catalogues, Internet, direct marketing, telesales. Or through wholesalers or agents, to retailers and customers. Or even setting up their own retail chain.

There are 7 marks for this part of the question, so you should spend 10 minutes answering it.

Syllabus reference – 3.10.

b. The next part follows on logically from (a), and looks at the **factors** you would take into account when making the decision.

Costs.
Market coverage.
Competitor activity.
Control.
Risk.
Amount of support needed.

There are 7 marks for this part of the question, so again you should spend 10 minutes answering it.

Syllabus reference – 3.11.

c. This final part looks at how you would measure the **effectiveness** of your channel decision. You should link the fact that you should return to the **measurable objectives** you set originally, and depending on these, you will measure:

Sales volume.
Sales value.
Profits.
Brand awareness.
New product trial.
Repeat purchases.

There are 6 marks for this part of the question, so you should spend 8 minutes answering it.

Syllabus reference – 3.10 and 3.11.

Question 3.

a. Again, no format is given. Remember the points made about format in the last question. In addition, in this question you are given a choice of organisation type, so long as you select one that offers a **service** rather than a product. Choose one that you are very familiar with. That will give you a good opportunity to illustrate all the points in both sections of the question. This could be **a bank, a hotel, a restaurant, a leisure centre, a hairdressers, etc**.

List all **7 Ps** in the **extended marketing mix**, and use each to illustrate how the needs and wants of customers might be met.

Product (or service).
Price.
Promotion.
Place.
People.
Process.
Physical evidence.

You may want to use a table to illustrate each element. Don't forget to keep using the example.

There are 12 marks for this part of the question, so you should spend roughly 18 minutes answering it.

Syllabus reference – 3.3, 3.13 and 3.14.

b. This part of the question leads on from the first. Look at various types of **Information and Communications Technology (ICT)** and how each contributes to the provision of **additional value to customers**.

Online information.

Online booking of appointments, accommodation, meals, etc.

Databases – for keeping customer information.

Better communication with staff to keep them updated.

Use of email contact (with permission) to advise of special offers or provide reminders.

There are 8 marks for this part of the question, so you should spend about 12 minutes answering it.

Syllabus reference – 3.15.

Question 4.

a. For the purposes of this question, you are employed by a **global car manufacturer**. Use your choice of firm to illustrate the various benefits marketing can offer to **both** the company **and** the customer.

Define marketing.

Benefits to consumers – choice, value, quality, safety.

Benefits to the company – meeting objectives, profits, sales growth, increased market share.

There are 12 marks for this part of the question, so you should spend 18 minutes answering it.

Syllabus reference – 1.2 and 4.2.

b. This section again follows on from the last, so you are still considering the **car market**.

Define **ethics** – moral principles, price discrimination, being honest in promotions.

Define **social responsibility** – emissions, pollution, depleting resources.

There are 8 marks for this part of the question, so you should spend around 12 minutes answering it.

Syllabus reference – 1.5.

Question 5.

a. This time you **manufacture TVs and hi-fi equipment**. The question asks you to **describe** and **illustrate**, so for each stage of the **marketing plan** that you identify, you need to give an **example** linked to the context of a **TV and hi-fi manufacturer**.

What is the **benefit** of planning?

Corporate goals.
Situation analysis.
Objectives.
Strategy.
Marketing mix.
Implementation.
Control.

There are 10 marks for this part of the question, so you should spend 15 minutes answering it.

Syllabus reference – 2.2 and 2.8.

b. This leads on from part (a) of the question. It is looking for the main considerations in **setting marketing budgets**.

Financial and resource requirements.

Methods of setting budgets – % sales, competitor based, objective and task.

Applies to all aspects of marketing – give examples linked to context.

There are 10 marks for this part of the question, so you should spend 15 minutes answering it.

Syllabus reference – 2.10.

Question 6.

a. This question is set in the context of a **small business**, specifically that of a **computer software house**. It goes on to explore the **product life cycle**, so it is worth remembering that in highly technical markets the product life cycle is quite short. It is looking for you to:

Define the product life cycle – you might draw a **diagram** of the product life cycle.

Describe the **marketing mix activities** and how they change at each of the following stages:

Introduction.
Growth.
Maturity.
Decline.

There are 10 marks for this part of the question, so you should spend 15 minutes answering it.

Syllabus reference – 3.5.

b. This leads on from the first section – so again is a software house. It looks at the influences on pricing decisions.

Internal – organisational objectives, pricing objectives, other mix variables.
External – costs, perceived value, demand, competition, regulation.

Again there are 10 marks for this part of the question, so you should spend 15 minutes answering it.

Syllabus reference – 3.8.

Question 7.

a. For this final question you can choose a **financial services** organisation, such as a **bank**, to illustrate your answer. Part (a) is all about **branding**.

Define branding.
Relate **benefits** to the **organisation**.
Relate **benefits** to **customers** of the bank.

There are 10 marks for this part of the question, so you should spend 15 minutes answering this section.

Syllabus reference – 3.6.

b. Part (b) is about **relationship marketing** and **customer retention**.

Define relationship marketing, using the bank as an example.
Compare to **transactional marketing**.
Identify benefits to buyers and sellers.

There are 10 marks for this part of the question, so you should spend 15 minutes answering it.

Syllabus reference – 1.6.

Appendix 5

Assessment guidance

There are two methods used for assessment of candidates – Examination <u>or</u> Continuous Assessment via projects.

The Chartered Institute of Marketing has traditionally used professional, externally set examinations as the means of assessment for the Certificate, Advanced Certificate and Postgraduate Diploma in Marketing. In 1995, at the request of industry, students and tutors, it introduced a continuously assessed route to two modules, one at Certificate level, and one at Advanced Certificate. With an increased emphasis on marketing practice, all modules are now open to assessment through examination or assessed project.

The information in this appendix will:

- Help you prepare for continuous assessment.
- Provide hints and tips to help you prepare for the examination.
- Manage your time effectively in preparing for assessment.

NB: Your tutor will inform you which method of assessment applies to your programme.

Preparing for continuous assessment

If you are being assessed by project you will be given a full brief for the assignment. This will include what you have to do, how it is to be presented, and the weighting of marks for each section. **YOU MUST READ THIS BEFORE YOU START, AND CHECK YOUR UNDERSTANDING OF WHAT IS BEING ASKED OF YOU WITH YOUR TUTOR.**

The assignment will consist of a number of tasks, each with their own weighting, so make sure you take account of this in your final presentation of the project.

The size of the project will be identified by a recommended word count. Check your final word count carefully, but remember quality is more important than quantity.

The assignment tasks will include a reflective statement. This requires you to identify what you have learned from the experience of undertaking the module, and how you have applied that learning to your job.

Questions you might want to consider in helping you write this reflective statement include: What was the most difficult part? How did you feel at the start of the exercise and how do you feel at the end? Did you achieve your objectives? If not, why not? What have you learned about yourself as you have worked through the module? How much of your learning have you been able to apply at work? Have you been able to solve any real work problems through the work you have done in your assignments?

This statement will be personal to you, and it should look forward to the points you have identified as needing work in the future. We should never stop learning. You should keep up this process of Continuous Professional Development as you go through your studies and your career, and hopefully you will have acquired the habit by the time you need to employ it to achieve Chartered Marketer status!

Examinations

Each subject differs slightly from the others, and the style of question will differ between module examinations. All are closed book examinations apart from **Analysis and Decision** (see below).

For all examinations, apart from **Marketing in Practice** (see below), the examination paper consists of two sections:

Part A – Mini-case, scenario or article

This section has a mini-case, scenario or article with compulsory questions. You are required to make marketing or sales decisions based on the information provided. You will gain credit for the decisions and recommendations you make on the basis of the analysis itself. This is a compulsory section of the paper designed to evaluate your practical marketing skills.

Part B – Examination questions

You will have a choice from a number of questions, and when answering those you select, ensure you understand the context of the question. Rough plans for each answer are strongly recommended.

The examination for **Marketing in Practice** differs in that the compulsory questions and examination questions are all linked to the mini-case and additional relevant information given, such as memos and reports.

The examination for **Analysis and Decision** is an open book examination and takes the form of a Case Study. This is mailed out 4 weeks before the examination and posted on the CIM student web site (www.cimvirtualinstitute.com) at the same time. Analysis and preparation should be completed during these four weeks. The questions asked in the examination will require strategic marketing decisions and actions. The question paper will also include additional unseen information about the Case Study.

CIM code of conduct for examinations

If being assessed by examination you will receive examination entry details, which will include a leaflet entitled "Rules for Examinations". You should read these carefully, as you will be penalised by CIM if you are in breach of any of these rules.

Most of the rules are common sense. For example, for closed book examinations you are not allowed to take notes or scrap paper into the examination room, and you must use the examination paper supplied to make rough notes and plans for your answer.

If you are taking the **Analysis and Decision** examination ensure that you do take your notes in with you, together with a copy of the Case Study.

Hints and tips

There are a number of places you can access information to help you prepare for your examination, if you are being assessed by this method. Your tutor will give you good advice, and exam hints and tips can also be found on the CIM student web site (www.cimvirtualinstitute.com).

Some fundamental points are listed below.

- Read the question carefully, and think about what is being asked before tackling the answer. The examiners are looking for knowledge, application and context. Refer back to the question to help you put your answer in the appropriate context. Do not just regurgitate theory.

- Consider the presentation style of your answer. For example, if you are asked to write a report, then use a report format with numbered headings and not an essay style.

- Structure – plan your answer to make it easy for the examiner to see the main points you are making.

- Timing – spread your time in proportion to the marks allocated, and ensure that all required questions are answered.

- Relevant examples – the examiners expect relevant theory to be illustrated by practical examples. These can be drawn from your own experience, reading of current journals and newspapers, or just your own observations. You could also visit "Hot Topics" on the CIM student web site to see discussions of topical marketing issues and practice.

Managing your time

What is effective time management? It is using wisely one of your most precious resources, **TIME**, to achieve your key goals. You need to be aware of how you spend your time each day. Set priorities, so you know what's important to you and what isn't. You need to establish goals for your study, work and family life, and plan how to meet those goals. Through developing these habits you will be better able to achieve the things that are important to you.

When study becomes one of your key goals you may find that, temporarily, something has to be sacrificed to find the time needed for reading, writing notes, writing up assignments, preparing for group assessment, etc. It helps to "get people on your side". Tell people that you are studying and ask for their support – this includes direct family, close friends and colleagues at work.

Time can just slip through your fingers if you don't manage it, and that's wasteful! When you are trying to balance the needs of family, social life, working life and study, there is a temptation to leave assignments until the deadline is nearly upon you. Don't give in to this temptation! Many students complain about the heavy workload towards the end of the course, when, in fact, they have had several months to work on assignments, and they have created this heavy workload themselves.

Knowing how to manage your time wisely can help you:

- Reduce pressure when you're faced with deadlines or a heavy schedule.
- Be more in control of your life by making better decisions about how to use your time.
- Feel better about yourself because you're using your full potential to achieve.
- Have more energy for the things you want or need to accomplish.
- Succeed more easily because you know what you want to do and what you need to do to achieve it.

Finally…

Remember to continue to apply your new skills within your job. Study and learning that is not applied just wastes your time, effort and money! Good luck with your studies!

Index

See also the Glossary on page 234.

You may find referring back to the Learning Outcomes and the Summary of Key Points at the beginning and end of each Session will aid effective use of the Index.

Only where subjects are relevantly discussed or defined are they indexed.

4Ps 67-68, 81-82, 88-89, 94, 164-165, 166-167, 169
5 markets model 21-22
7Ps 19-20, 52, 68-70, 142-143, 177-180

Adidas 103
advertising 123, 125, 129-130
agents 109
Ansoff matrix 30-31
APIC 32

b2b marketing 168
  – buying decisions 128-129
background reading 7
banks 143
banner ads 129-130
Barnardo's 170-171
BCG (Boston Consulting Group matrix) 84
brand awareness 157
branding 87-88
budgets 54-56
business analysis 85
buying behaviour 126-129

channels 109-117
  – conflict 111-112
commercialisation 85
communities 130
company resources 125
competition 99

competitors 113
concentrated marketing 66
concept testing 85
contingency arrangements 31
convenience goods 77
co-ordinating plans 19
cost 113
cost analysis 157
costs 98-99, 114
CRM (Customer Relationship Management) 21-22, 141
customer focus 17
customer loyalty 124
customer satisfaction levels 157
customer value 15-16

databases 153
delivery 114-145
differentiated marketing 66
direct routes 110
distribution 100, 109-117
distributors 109
DRIP (Differentiate, Remind, Inform, Persuade) 123, 129
DRTV (Direct Response TV) 129, 155

e-marketing 153-154, 178-180
e-shopping 117-118, 125
ethics 20-21
extended marketing mix 68-70

FMCG (Fast Moving Consumer Goods) 131, 168-169
franchising 115

grey market 57-59

heterogeneity 140

ICT (Information and Communications Technology) 152-161
idea generation 85
innovation 116
inseparability 139-140
intangibility 139
Interflora 71-72
intermediaries 110
international marketing 176-178
Internet 111, 117, 153-154
interstitials 130
Intranets 131

Just in Time (JIT) 114

key skills 4

legal factors 100, 114
logistics 110

management control 30
management structures 52-53
manager 20
market demand 99
market location 113
market penetration 101
market size 86
market skimming 101
marketing – definitions 11-13, 14
marketing audit 33-35
marketing communications planning framework 32

marketing effectiveness 156-157
marketing environment audit 33
marketing function audit 35
marketing in different contexts 163-714
marketing mix 52, 64-72, 81-82, 94, 152-156
marketing models 8-9
marketing organisation audit 34
marketing orientation 16
marketing plan 43-60, 49-52
marketing planning 29
marketing productivity audit 35
marketing research 36
marketing strategy audit 34
marketing systems audit 35
monitoring and controlling 56
mosaic group 181
Müller yoghurt 89-90

new product development 85-87
Nike 103
not-for-profit marketing 166

objectives 43-46, 125
opt-in emails 131
organisational planning 30
organisational structure 53-54
out-of-town retailing 116
ownership 140

packaging 88-89, 131-132
people 143-144 – *see also* 7Ps
perishability 140
permission marketing 15
personal selling 125
PEST 35, 49
physical evidence 143 – *see also* 7Ps
place 109-121 – *see also* 4Ps, 7Ps

Index

planning models 31-32
PLC (Product Life Cycle) 79-83, 84, 94
portals 131
positioning 64-66
price 97-107 *see also* 4Ps, 7Ps
pricing decisions 97-98
pricing policies 100-101
pricing tactics 101
  – product line 101
  – optional product 102
  – product bundle 102
  – cost-plus 102
  – demand-based 102
  – competitor parity 102
  – psychological 102
primary research 37
process 143 – *see also* 7Ps
Procter & Gamble 22-23
product 77-95
  – core product 78-79
  – actual product 78-79
  – augmented product 79
  – product mix 83
  – product policy 83-4
  – product benefits 93
  – product characteristics 113
  – product costs 98-9
  – product development 85 – *see also* 4Ps, 7Ps, pricing tactics
promotional mix 123-137 – *see also* 4Ps, 7Ps
public relations 124, 125-126
purchase decisions 126-129

qualitative research 36
quantitative research 36

re-buy 168
relationship marketing 21-22, 141
research 19, 37
resource allocation 30
retailers 110

sales analysis 157
sales orientation 13
sales promotion 124
SALT (Same as Last Time) 55
screening ideas 85
secondary research 37
segmentation 46-50, 57-59, 64-66
  – criteria 47
  – consumer 47-48
  – business to business 49
service marketing 139-150
shopping goods 77
situation analysis 49-50
Skoda 133-135, 157-158
SMART objectives 44-47, 50, 56
SMEs (Small to Medium sized Enterprises) 164
  – buying decisions 128-129
social responsibility 20-21
SOSTAC 32
SOSTTMMMM 32
strategy 50-51
SWOT 35

targeting 64-66
technology 155-156
test marketing 85

undifferentiated marketing 65

web sites 5-6, 111, 129-131
wholesalers 109

233

(Planning process)

M — mission ⎫ where are we now?
A — audit   ⎭
O — objectives ⎫ where do we
S — strategy   ⎭ want to be?
T — tactics   ⎫ How to
I — Implementation ⎭ get there?
C — control — how to ensure arrival